Wrong and Dangerous

Wrong and Dangerous

Ten Right-Wing Myths about Our Constitution

GARRETT EPPS

ROWMAN & LITTLEFIELD PUBLISHERS, INC.
Lanham • Boulder • New York • Toronto • Plymouth, UK

Published by Rowman & Littlefield Publishers, Inc.
A wholly owned subsidiary of The Rowman & Littlefield Publishing Group, Inc.
4501 Forbes Boulevard, Suite 200, Lanham, Maryland 20706
www.rowman.com

10 Thornbury Road, Plymouth PL6 7PP, United Kingdom

Distributed by National Book Network

British Library Cataloguing in Publication Information Available

Library of Congress Cataloging-in-Publication Data

Epps, Garrett.
  Wrong and dangerous : ten right-wing myths about our constitution / Garrett
Epps.
    p. cm.
  Includes bibliographical references and index.
  ISBN 978-1-4422-1676-1 (cloth : alk. paper) — ISBN 978-1-4422-1678-5
(electronic)
  1. Constitutional law—United States—Interpretation and construction.
  2. Constitutional law—United States—Popular works. 3. Constitutional
amendments—United States—Popular works. 4. Conservatism—United States.
  5. Law—United States—Interpretation and construction. I. Title.
  KF4550.E66 2012 342.7302
  342.7302—dc23 EPP 2012012355

∞™ The paper used in this publication meets the minimum requirements of
American National Standard for Information Sciences—Permanence of Paper for
Printed Library Materials, ANSI/NISO Z39.48-1992.

Printed in the United States of America

This book is for all my students—young and old; left and right; past, present, and future. Have fun storming the castle!

A little patience, and we shall see the reign of witches pass over, their spells dissolve, and the people, recovering their true sight, restore their government to its true principles.

—Thomas Jefferson, 1798

Contents

Acknowledgments

Katrina Vanden Heuvel, editor of *The Nation*, commissioned me to re-count my day in "Constitution school" under the title "Stealing the Constitution," which began my work on far-right "constitutionalism." Steve Farley (D-28) of the Arizona House of Representatives invited me to speak to a group of legislators at the Arizona State Capitol in March 2011. It was for that speech that I first came up with the (now much altered) "Ten Myths" list. Bob Cohn and John Gould of atlantic.com, superb editors, published the myths list as a series of columns in the summer of 2011. Kit Rachlis, editor of *The American Prospect*, patiently helped me turn my thoughts on campaign finance and civic equality into a longer essay. Josh Swanner and Taylor Novak, students at the University of Baltimore School of Law, served as research assistants, proofreaders, editors, and joke providers for this book. Bob Deans, an old comrade from Southern politics and journalism, offered not only encouragement but also genuine help, and introduced me to Jonathan Sisk, the patient editor at Rowman & Littlefield who undertook to publish the book. Rafe Sagalyn graciously provided general counsel on book contracts. My colleague Elizabeth Samuels was a sounding board, offered encouragement, and was a general force for good, as was David Ignatius. Kent Greenfield, Tamara Piety, and Adam Winkler read sections of the book and offered suggestions. Ian Millhiser of the Center for American Progress, whose columns monitoring the follies of the Right are a constant inspiration, underscored the urgency of the task by inviting me to take part in a panel at CAP on "What Happens if the Tea Party Wins?" Finally, my writing buddy for forty years, on and off, Lynn Darling, helped me meet my deadlines. Little birds are writing interesting books.

Introduction:
Stealing the Constitution

In October 2012 I spent a full day in a windowless church basement in Northern Virginia, as a student at a seminar on "The Substance and Meaning of the Constitution." My day job is constitutional scholar. I have spent the last twenty years studying the text and history of the Constitution, and teaching students about the ways in which courts have applied our fundamental law to the practical problems of our society. But I have to confess I knew nothing about the history I learned at Constitution school.

The "truth" about the Constitution is this: God wrote it. He handed it down to Moses, who applied it to govern the people of Israel. This divine law was carried from ancient Israel to Northern Europe after the Assyrian Conquest in 720 BCE by the famous "lost tribes" of Israel. After much wandering, these chosen people settled in the British Isles, where they took the name "Anglo-Saxon." They ruled their medieval kingdom by the law of Moses, but its purity was lost after the Norman Conquest in 1066 CE. The Founding Fathers of the new United States, inspired by the Lord of Hosts, wrote the Constitution to restore His Anglo-Saxon kingdom.

Since it is God's will that Americans live like medieval Saxons, it shouldn't surprise anyone that virtually all of modern American life and government is unconstitutional: Social Security, the Federal Reserve, the Environmental Protection Agency, the Civil Rights Act of 1964, hate crime laws—illegal inventions of a people who have been led astray by false prophets. The trouble began with the Civil War, a needless conflict in which the wrong side won. Slaves were happy and carefree in slavery.

1

Racism was caused by pushy Northern abolitionists. State governments are not required to observe the Bill of Rights. The very idea of separation between church and state is a pernicious myth; the First Amendment's religion clauses establish "nondenominational" Christianity as "the religion of America."

The seminar I attended was organized by the National Center for Constitutional Studies, nestled securely in the metropolis of Malta, Idaho (2010 Census population: 177, 98 percent of them white). The center is the brainchild of the late W. Cleon Skousen, a former Salt Lake City police chief (he once raided the mayor's regular poker game) and FBI agent.

Students paid $50 each for the seminar. They received a carefully prepared workbook with fill-in-the-blank questions such as "Events since 1913 have demonstrated that the original *intent* of the Founders in setting up the Senate as a legislative guardian has been largely emasculated by the Seventeenth Amendment." Students also had the chance to buy the Center's expensively produced textbook, *The Making of America: The Substance and Meaning of the Constitution*, which explains Skousen's ideas in greater detail. The long section on slavery in this textbook has been amended since the 1980s, when the Center attempted to persuade California to adopt it as an official high school textbook. They abandoned the attempt after news reports alerted people that the book referred to black children as "picaninnies." Now it carefully indicates where the word once appeared by the use of brackets: "If [negro children] ran naked it was generally from choice, and when the white boys had to put on shoes and go away to school they were likely to envy the freedom of their colored playmates." [1]

The instructor was Lester Pearce, an Arizona justice of the peace. Pearce is the brother of former Arizona state senator Russell Pearce, author of Arizona's notorious anti-immigrant law, SB 1070. Lester tended to wander off into discussions of how he refuses to comply with court rules requiring him to allow defendants in his court to speak Spanish. Arizona's "open carry" weapons laws, which permit citizens to strap pistols to their hips and stroll downtown, would, he predicted, save Arizona when the United Nations sent its blue-helmet troops into the state to enforce bogus "human-rights" laws. Pearce admitted that much of what he does in Justice Court doesn't exactly follow the law as laid down by higher courts, whose decisions he is technically supposed to follow. But those court decisions are just other judges' opinions, he said. He doesn't really need to pay attention; he has his own views. Pearce got rapt attention from the fifty people in the audience, although one boy near me spent his time on a detailed sketch of an assault rifle.

My ordeal would have little importance if the seminar I attended were an isolated gathering of cranks. Many of the myths Pearce was purveying have floated around in the American unconscious for years. I used to run across them in the hills and hollows of rural Oregon back in the heyday of the militia movement. But the NCCS "school" is actually part of a growing movement. Every weekend, NCCS instructors fly around the country to teach the glories of the Anglo-Saxon Constitution. The *Washington Post* estimated in 2009 that the Center sponsored as many as 180 classes around the country, not counting the one-day public events conducted by NCCS on patriotic holidays. The session I attended was sponsored by local Tea Party groups and by the county Republican committee.

The NCCS is far from the only source of far-right mythology about the Constitution. Turn on any AM radio talk station, or Fox News Channel, or C-SPAN. The far-right myth of the Constitution is being systematically mainstreamed.

Americans today are frightened and disoriented. Since 2000, our society has been through a series of shocks: the misfire and ham-fisted resolution of the 2000 presidential election; the September 11 attacks; the disastrous war in Iraq; the erosion of civil liberties at home; the economic collapse of 2008; the cynical bailout of America's richest banks and corporations; unemployment and widespread foreclosures for ordinary Americans.

What has gone wrong?

In the midst of uncertainty, people are turning to the Constitution for tools to deal with crisis. The Constitution is what makes Americans who we are. All federal and state officials—from the president to state JPs like Lester Pearce—swear an oath to support and defend it. Americans hope that the document will show them the way out of the dangerous thicket we find ourselves in. The Far Right—the toxic coalition of Fox News talking heads, radio hosts, angry "patriot" groups, and power-hungry Tea Party politicians—is feeding them mythology and lies.

Take the rise of NCCS: The Center's crazed ideology leapt into national prominence when Glenn Beck began touting its "educational" programs on his TV show and his online "Beck University." Civic groups, school districts, and even some city governments across the country have been persuaded to sponsor daylong seminars by the "nonpartisan" NCCS; its speakers are visiting high schools to distribute pocket copies of the Constitution. NCCS is mounting a major drive to have its materials adopted as official curriculum in schools around the country—roughly the equivalent of requiring the Book of Genesis as a biology textbook. Skousen's massive "guide" to the Constitution, *The Making of America: The Substance and Meaning of the Constitution*, has ranked as high as No. 4 in the past year on Amazon's list of best-selling titles on the Constitution.

NCCS is far from alone in peddling far-right constitutional mythology as fact. A broad, energetic campaign is underway to do for our understanding of the Constitution what the Right has done to global warming and evolution—that is, to wipe out the facts and substitute a partisan myth.

We've all heard conservative orators denouncing the Affordable Care Act, the new health insurance law. They claim it's unconstitutional to require taxpayers either to buy health insurance or to pay a tax penalty. To most constitutional lawyers, that position would have seemed radical only a few years ago. But by comparisons with some of the new claims conservatives are advancing, it's positively timid.

In fact, it's difficult to understate how extreme this emerging right-wing picture of the Constitution is. Popular authors Thomas Woods Jr. and Kevin Gutzman, in their book *Who Killed the Constitution?*, argue that racial segregation in schools was perfectly constitutional, and that *Brown v. Board of Education*, which struck down the Southern "separate but equal" school system, is illegitimate. Newly elected Senator Mike Lee of Utah has endorsed state "nullification" of the health care law—a doctrine that until now was associated with Southern racist resistance to desegregation. Representative Ron Paul demands that "we end all the unconstitutional federal departments including the Department of Energy, Education, Agriculture, Commerce, Health and Human Services, Homeland Security, and Labor."[2] Fox News Channel commentator Andrew Napolitano attacks Democrats for supporting "federal child labor laws, the Clean Air Act, the EPA, and the Department of Transportation . . . none of them is even arguably authorized by the Constitution."[3]

At the beginning of the 112th Congress, far-right Republican Representative Michele Bachmann set up a "Constitution school" for new members of Congress. She invited Napolitano to lecture to the students.

Justice Antonin Scalia (in other contexts a stickler for the separation of powers) also agreed to join Bachmann's faculty.

Scalia's injudicious involvement with House Republicans underscores another disturbing fact. Conservative federal judges are increasingly adopting the rhetoric and ideas of the hard Right; in the process, they are casting aside the traditional ethics of judging that required them to at least act nonpartisan. Scalia, in fact, is an old duck-hunting partner of former vice president Dick Cheney. In his public appearances, he sounds more and more like a conservative politician and less and less like a mere judge. Citizens who resent the Court's clumsy intervention in the 2000 election should "get over it," he once said.[4] He managed to find himself in South Carolina on the eve of the 2012 Republican primary, and told citizens offended by the damage the *Citizens United* decision has done to politics that all they have to do is "turn off the TV."[5]

Scalia is the soul of modesty compared to his fellow conservative, Clarence Thomas. Thomas tells conservative audiences that he and his wife Virginia—a Tea Party activist who was outspoken against the health care law—"believe the same things," and that his liberal critics are trying to undermine the Supreme Court by even questioning his impartiality.[6] Both Scalia and Thomas have spoken to secret conferences of far-right fat-cat donors. Thomas has accepted an all-expense-paid trip to address a Koch brothers conference, and has accepted lavish gifts from far-right Texas millionaire Harlan Crow, a funder of "Swiftboat Veterans for Truth" in the 2004 election cycle. Thomas and Scalia appeared as guests at a dinner hosted by two corporate law firms—on the same day that the justices had met in secret to decide whether to hear those firms' challenge to overturn the Patient Protection and Affordable Care Act.

Justice Samuel A. Alito has been a speaker at fundraising events for the virulently right-wing *American Spectator*. Until the rise of the conservative Court, any of these activities would have been considered a shocking violation of a judge's duty to refrain from political activity and to refrain from any behavior that would raise questions about his or her objectivity. Increasingly, they are the norm for justices who no longer hide their partisan views.

It's easy to understand why conservative politicians and judges are trying to align their political program with a strained reading of the Constitution: it's the only way they can achieve their political goals. Senate Republican leader Mitch McConnell recently demanded a balanced-budget amendment to the Constitution, designed to cripple the federal government, because, he said, "We've tried persuasion. We've tried negotiations. We've tried elections. Nothing has worked."[7] Conservative politicians like to claim that America is a center-right country, but in fact, people want the good things an energetic government can do. Social Security and Medicare; environmental protection; consumer safety regulation—all these things are popular. The people, those idiots, keep voting for programs they like.

The people must be stopped.

So the Right is seeking to win by changing the rules. A growing number of conservative lawmakers and commentators claim that the "original intent" of the Constitution's framers and the views of the right wing of the Republican Party are one and the same. Progressive, democratically enacted policy choices are unconstitutional. In their radical new reading, the Constitution does not set down the rules for running a government, but instead decides all questions of policy. If something is not mentioned in the Constitution, it's unconstitutional. "Nowhere in the Constitution do we read the words, 'the government shall provide for health care,'" complains Representative Virginia Foxx (R-NC). "In fact, the words 'health care' are nowhere in the Constitution." Senator Tom Coburn (R-OK) echoes this wrong-headed argument.[8] Yes, "health care" doesn't appear in the constitution, but the Right's astonishment at this is entirely pretended. The words "Centers for Disease Control," "cancer research," "space program," "American flag," and "interstate highway system" are also missing. That's because the men who wrote the Constitution had never heard those words; beyond that, it's because they spent their time laying out a system of government, and left the question of what *policies* that government would follow to future generations. That's what they would have called self-government.

Today's "constitutionalists" aren't even content to distort the words of the Constitution. They want to amend it in many places to subvert the system it has created. The Right is determined to write a federal marriage amendment into the Constitution, making it impossible for any state to allow same-sex marriage. A human life amendment is also on their wish list. Many Tea Party groups are demanding a new constitutional convention to strip Congress of its current powers. House majority leader Eric Cantor supports a constitutional amendment to permit the state legislatures to repeal federal laws. Most Republicans support a "balanced-budget" amendmcnt that would permanently cripple our ability to finance an adequate federal budget.

Why has the Right done such a good job of projecting its invented "Constitution"? The past decade has done much to shake the public's faith in our institutions. Under President George W. Bush, the federal government began to conduct surveillance, eavesdrop on private conversations, intercept email, and imprison foreigners and citizens in military prisons. It was Bush, not liberals, who most aggressively created an overreaching federal government. Bush lied to the public about the threat from Iraq and bungled the war he started. Finally, his economic policies wrecked the economy, and when the structure began to fail, his government made sure the suffering would fall only on ordinary people.

Economic inequality, which has been on the rise since the 1980s, has gone into overdrive with the recession that began in 2008. The bank and corporate bailouts of that year have been one of the most corrosive events in American history: they crystallize perfectly the ordinary person's sense that the system is rigged against them and in favor of the wealthy elite. Because of the timing of the bailouts—just before the inauguration of a new administration—Barack Obama has become identified in the public mind with bailouts and banks as well. At the same time, the pace of social change has disoriented ordinary Americans. The Far Right has come up with a proposed solution to the problem: it wants to abolish the twentieth century.

One unifying theme of the diverse Tea Party groups is their opposition to immigration; their fear of foreigners has been worsened, I think, by the election of an American president with black skin and a foreign-sounding name. And the president has failed to put forward an alternative economic or social vision that would offer confidence and hope to those hit hardest by the recession.

Truly, the center in America has not held. As Ian Millhiser of the Center for American Progress has explained,[9] the failure of the Bush administration discredited the conservative elites. Traditional pro-business Republicans now carry the stain of the bailout; the "neo-conservatives" who staffed the Bush foreign policy and defense apparatus were the architects of the war in Iraq. America has always had a strain of conservatism that was thoughtful, grounded in history, and respectful of tradition. As a progressive, I often disagree with these conservatives about the nature of democracy, the wisdom of economic regulation, the proper extent of the Commerce Power, and the proper role of equality. But I seldom thought—as I do more and more often today—that when engaging conservative arguments I was talking to people who simply did not live on the same planet as the rest of us.

Since 2008, lunatics have taken over the conservative asylum. The traditional conservatives have found themselves talking to the air—witness the defeat of a conservative figure like Utah senator Robert Bennett by Tea Party darling Mike Lee. Dozens of the new Tea Party Caucus House Members showed they were perfectly willing to risk worldwide economic collapse by allowing the United States to default on its debt. Republican presidential candidate Rick Perry attacked Republican Fed chairman—and former Bush staffer—Ben Bernanke as "almost treasonous" for his efforts to prevent a double-dip recession.[10] In the absence of sane, experienced leadership, what is called "movement conservatism" has been hijacked by a distinctly motley crew of far-right mouthpieces.

The NCCS, for example, clearly springs out of a certain kind of conservative religious politics. It blends those with the old-style Cold War ultraconservatism of groups like the John Birch Society, which regarded all postwar American history as the triumph of Communist treason. (The society's founder, Robert Welch, once called Dwight Eisenhower "a conscious, dedicated agent of the Communist conspiracy.")

But note the legend about Anglo-Saxons and the Ten Lost Tribes. That doesn't come from ordinary Christian conservatism, or from Mormon fundamentalism. It ought to set off a warning announcement: "You are now entering deepest Crazy Town." The Anglo-Saxon legend is the remnant of a movement called "British Israelism," which arose in the nineteenth century to argue that the people of Britain, not the world's Jews, were the "chosen people" of the Christian Bible. "Israelism" arose at the same time as the burgeoning of the worldwide British Empire. Not surprisingly, the idea that white Britons were God's chosen people made it okay for them to rule nonwhite people around the world: that was the divine plan.

But it also was a strong justification for virulent anti-Semitism. Jews, in the "Israelite" literature, weren't actually descended from the Hebrews of the Old Testament; they were fraudulent interlopers. Some "Israelists" claimed they were actually "Khazars," descendants of a Turkic people whose ruling elite converted to Judaism in the eighth century BCE. Things got worse when "Israelism," as is documented by scholar Michael Barkun in his book *Religion and the Racist Right: The Origins of the Christian Identity Movement*,[11] jumped across the Atlantic in the twentieth century and became the basis of a white-supremacist brand of "Christianity"—the "Identity religion"—headquartered in the Pacific Northwest. "Identity" Christianity is an inspiration behind violent vigilante groups like the Aryan Nation and the Hutaree Militia.

The Cold War–era Far Right contributes the idea of a domestic "enemy," which is very powerful in the "constitutionalist" movement. American society spent more than two generations in a deadly competition with the Communist world. The American Right during that time convinced itself that American government and society had been infiltrated—like the fictional Santa Mira, California, in Don Siegel's film *Invasion of the Body Snatchers*—by an alien force, in this case a Fifth Column of Communists and "sympathizers." The end of the Cold War left a lot of the Far Right bereft. Who was the enemy now?

Well, turns out it's Democrats. Michele Bachmann once called for an investigation of Congress to determine which members are "anti-American." "We have a lot of domestic enemies, enemies of the Constitution," Representative Paul Broun (R-GA) said on the floor of the House not long ago. "This House is overrun with domestic enemies of the Constitution and the Senate's full of a bunch of them also."[12] Representative Allen West recently said, "I believe there's about 78 to 81 members of the Democrat Party who are members of the Communist Party. . . . It's called the Congressional Progressive Caucus."[13] In the new post–Cold War world of paranoia, it doesn't take much—support for Medicare, maybe—to qualify as a dangerous traitor.

Mixed in with the John Birch and white-supremacist strains of conservatism is a persistent nostalgia for the Confederate States of America. Since the day after Appomattox, voices in our society have been insisting that the South, not the North, had it right all along. The Civil War, in their revisionist history, had nothing to do with slavery and everything to do with the meddling North's hatred of the noble, agrarian South. Slavery, in this version, wasn't such a big deal. (Note the echoes of that argument in *The Making of America*.) It might have been slightly regrettable, but generous Southerners would have ended it voluntarily in just a generation or two, or three, or at least sometime when they felt like it. The war was really about "states' rights," and the refusal of the Yankee juggernaut to respect the "original intent" of the Constitution.

Abraham Lincoln, in this retelling, was a tyrant who wrecked the Constitution out of vindictive hatred for the South. "The sum of Lincoln's constitutionalism seems to have been 'whatever I favor is constitutional,'" writes far-right historian Kevin R. C. Gutzman in *The Politically Incorrect Guide™ to the Constitution.* Gutzman also insists that the South was fighting for government "of the people, by the people, for the people."[14]

This "slavery nostalgia" wing of the Right is the source of the current vogue for state "nullification" of federal law. They claim that "nullification" is the handiwork of Thomas Jefferson and James Madison, whose Virginia and Kentucky Resolutions protested the Alien and Sedition Acts of 1798. They have misread and misrepresented those resolutions. But in any case, the 1798 idea of "nullification" was a good deal less radical than the current version being peddled to red-state legislatures; at any rate, the original version has been dead since the Andrew Jackson administration. Today's "nullifiers" find their true intellectual inspiration in the Southern "massive resistance" movement against *Brown v. Board of Education.* That "nullification" was the brainchild of a few segregationist ideologues and inspired school closings and racial violence across the South during the 1950s. The roots of this strain of contemporary far-right discourse, like those of the "Ten Lost Tribes" idea, lie directly in white supremacy and racism.

These echoes of the Cold War and of racism are not the only notes in the cacophony of conservative ideas clamoring for acceptance. Equally important are the ideas of the Christian right. For generations, fundamentalist Christians have believed that America is "their" country, founded and designed as a "Christian nation." (By that term, most of them mean a "Protestant Christian" nation.) The Christian right's in-house "historian," David Barton, is the spokesman for this brand of constitutional mythology. Barton, who has no training in history, has produced a flood of books designed to demonstrate that the Founding Fathers were devout Christians who intended the new nation to be run by and for believers. We'll look in more detail at some of his claims later. The important point for now is that his half-baked views are taken with utter seriousness by Republican politicians. The Bush campaign in 2004 sent him on a tour of small American towns, where he explained to groups of Protestant pastors that the "original intent" of the Founding Fathers was for churches to be heavily involved in politics. In the current election cycle, he has advised both former House Speaker Newt Gingrich and Representative Michele Bachmann.[15]

Bachmann herself, a graduate of Oral Roberts Law School (now Regent Law School, owned by religious broadcaster Pat Robertson), is a product of this Christian-right tradition. (She briefly suggested that Barton join the "faculty" of her "school" for new members of Congress.) Fundamentalists and conservative evangelicals have in the past generation spawned an entire universe of Christian schools, colleges, law schools, and think-tanks to spread their version of history within a movement that has become almost completely sealed off from any competing vision of American history and law. Much of its history is distorted or invented, but in the airless world of the Christian right, it is protected from serious challenge.

Another strand of the current conservative brand of "constitutionalism" comes from the libertarian philosophy that has sprung up since World War II. Libertarians argue that the very existence of government and the state is unnecessary and immoral. Their ideas stem from the work of Austrian economists Ludwig von Mises and F. A. Hayek, who argued that an active government leads inevitably to the loss of personal freedom.

Mingling with the "Austrian economics" school of libertarianism is the homegrown strain popularized by novelist Ayn Rand during the 1950s in novels like *The Fountainhead* and *Atlas Shrugged.* Rand was more a moralist than an economist; in her view of the world, all human progress is the result of individual human beings pursuing their own individual self-interest. Cooperative endeavor of any kind—"collectivism"—is wrong-headed and immoral. The claims of human sympathy—such ideas as community responsibility and altruism—are not just blather; they are dangerous tools used by the weak to batten on the strong. Taxation in and of itself is robbery of property that strong individuals have assembled for themselves. The only valid moral principle is that each individual should provide for him- or herself and leave others free to do so, or to starve. (Think of the scattered voices cheering last winter when a news reporter at a Republican presidential debate asked Ron Paul whether uninsured patients should be allowed to bleed to death in emergency rooms.)

To a libertarian, any government program is suspicious, and any program to help citizens with problems like old-age pensions, health care, childhood nutrition, or racial discrimination is a profound social affront. To them, a properly run society would have almost no public sector. It would be instead what the libertarians call a "night watchman" state—

probably only a military to protect the nation from foreign threats and a law enforcement apparatus to protect private property against theft.

A number of legal scholars in the past twenty years have begun to advance the idea that the Constitution is really a libertarian document, or if it isn't it should be. The current argument against the federal health care statute comes from libertarian ideas. In their analysis, government programs—even ones that benefit the whole society—are *by definition* trespasses against "liberty," which means solely the right to stand or fall completely on one's own. (The idea that the opposition comes from the "individual mandate" is a smokescreen; no matter what kind of health care statute Congress passed, the arguments would be the same.)

Sincere libertarians, like Ron Paul, have a certain goofy charm. Many of them are quite sincere about wanting to think through the implications of their economic ideas and apply them consistently. But there are three problems with the role of libertarianism in the current debate.

First, with its radical individualism, its contempt for community, and its prejudice against government, libertarianism is a relatively new school of thought. Founded in the twentieth century, it has absolutely nothing to do with the ideas behind the U.S. Constitution. Libertarians embrace mythology when they claim that Washington, Madison, Franklin, or any of the other Founders "intended" to write Hayek's ideas into a document created in 1787. Eighteenth-century "small-r" republicans like the Founders believed strongly in concepts that today's libertarians hate: community service, economic equality, the common good. Governments in the Founding period frequently intervened in the marketplace in ways that would give Hayek and von Mises fits.

The Constitution doesn't require eighteenth-century-style economics; it would certainly *permit* the people to enact a libertarian system if they chose, but there is no reasonable case that it *forbids* them to choose other systems, including one like the current one in which government regulates the economy in the interest of health and safety and provides help for citizens needing it. Yet, increasingly, that "original intent" argument is the claim that some "constitutionalists" are making. As a matter of history and text, it's as silly as Barton's claims about a "Christian nation," or Skousen's about the Ten Lost Tribes.

Second, for all the invocations of "liberty," a true "night watchman state" is one most of us wouldn't want to live in. A huge industrial society without economic regulation, protections for workers against danger and

exploitation, or environmental controls would be worse than unlivable—
it would collapse fairly quickly into chaos. Most of us would experience
very little "liberty" without laws to protect the weak against the strong,
or provide emergency assistance for victims of storms, floods, fires, and
earthquakes.

Third, the deployment of libertarian ideas by the contemporary Far
Right is deceptive. "Liberty" in a truly all-encompassing sense is not what
the Far Right is after. The government they envision retains sweeping
power over our lives—to direct our spiritual development, to control
not only whom we marry but also how we behave in our bedrooms, to
dictate our choices about premarital sex, abortion, and contraception. If
their ideas triumph, we risk finding ourselves in what we might call "au-
thoritarian libertarianism," a world in which government is forbidden to
help us find health care but free to regulate our family and sexual lives, to
"suggest" prayers, and to tell us what we can and can't say. And, of course,
much of the Republican Right is strongly behind new legal provisions allowing military and national-security agencies to jail Americans without
charge or trial.

As you can see, the Far Right's ideas about the Constitution aren't
historically accurate, workable, or even coherent. One thing holds them
together—the desire, more or less explicit, to repeal the entire twentieth
century. At first glance, it's an appealing idea: wars, totalitarianism, the rise
of nuclear weapons—what's to love about the last century? But it turns out
those aren't the things the Right objects to. Instead, one conception brings
together the libertarian intellectuals, traditionalists, right-wing Christian,
and Tea Partiers: an absolute hatred of the Progressive Era of American
politics.

Most Americans don't see the world in highly politicized, ideological
terms. To them, it may seem confusing that the Right focuses so much
fury on an era in American life that is seldom discussed today. But focus
they do. *How Progressives Rewrote the Constitution* is the title of an influential tract by Richard Epstein, the most influential scholarly proponent of
a libertarian reading of the Constitution.[16] At a far less exalted intellectual
level, Texas governor Rick Perry warns darkly that "since the dawn of
the so-called Progressive movement over a century ago, liberals have used
every tool at their disposal—including, notably, the Supreme Court—to
wage a gradual war on the Constitution and the American way of life, with
very little effective opposition from conservatives."[17] Tea Party activists

sell T-shirts emblazoned *1913. WORST. YEAR. EVER.* That's because the people—those idiots!—amended the Constitution in 1913 to allow a progressive income tax and direct election of senators. Congress also created the Federal Reserve Bank System. And Woodrow Wilson became president. "It was truly a pernicious time for freedom," writes Andrew Napolitano.[18] Everything since 1913 has been a combination of conspiracy and man-made disaster.

It's a curious idea, because among other things, wiping out the past hundred years means wiping out what is called the American Century. Since 1913, the United States has (1) become the greatest economic power on earth; (2) built a standard of living never equaled anywhere, at any time; (3) expanded democracy and citizenship to forbid racial and sex discrimination; (4) rallied the free peoples of the globe to defeat Nazism; (5) blunted the threat of Communism without war; (6) sparked an era of technological progress that included the first manned expedition to the moon and the transformative creation of the personal computer and the Internet; and (7) flowered culturally with great literature, art, cinema, and music that are now read, seen, watched, and heard with admiration everywhere in the world.

So what went so all-fired wrong in 1913? The true horror is that the idea of popular democracy, as in election of senators, finally became the dominant ideal of American politics. The year is a symbol of the modernization of our country and our system. Sleepy economic backwaters began to join into the national system. The federal government began to protect working people and consumers from the excesses of monopoly capitalism. Women began to vote, and then to demand equal rights in the home and outside of it. Racial minorities rejected their second-class status. New religious groups created greater religious and cultural pluralism. New immigration streams transformed America demographically, powering industrial growth.

Change happened. And much of it was good. But the new Far Right wants all of it gone. "I want my country back" is a common cry from the Tea Party ranks. The country they want "back," however, is one that never existed, where God-fearing, gun-toting families prospered without government assistance, and god-like businessmen ran their empires with no worry about labor unions, environmental protection, or human equality. That today's "constitutionalists" want to bring it "back" is a devastating comment on their underlying values.

The Right's ideas are not particularly good ones, and they aren't particularly coherent, but they are being trumpeted far and wide—in the halls of Congress, on the presidential campaign trail, on talk radio and right-wing TV. The Right is richly funded, with its own TV network, Fox News Channel; its own global daily, the *Wall Street Journal*; its own dedicated New York publisher, Henry Regnery & Co.; its own Minister of Information, Rush Limbaugh; its own magazines like the *Weekly Standard*; think-tanks like the Heritage Foundation and the Cato Institute; and even a book club. Right-wing millionaires and foundations have deeply penetrated American universities as well, endowing chairs in specific elements of economic and political thought that usually seem to go to academic spokesmen for the Right.

And all that is simply the apparatus of the economic-libertarian Right. In addition, the religious Right has also perfected an alternative communications system, operating through churches, church schools, Christian broadcast outlets, book publishers, and websites, in which its version of history and law need never encounter an outside challenge. This whole apparatus is what journalism scholars Kathleen Hall Jameson and Joseph N. Cappella have christened "the echo chamber."[19] All in all, it's a formidable propaganda machine.

The progressive and mainstream side of the argument hasn't fought back as effectively as it could. Sometimes it seems that Democrats and progressives don't want to engage the constitutional argument. Barack Obama was at one time a constitutional law professor, but as president he has not been willing to call out his critics for the claims they make about the Constitution. Mainstream working journalists often seem uneducated about the Constitution, and repeat right-wing claims as if they were credible or even obviously true.

Some of the responsibility for this passive response lies with progressive and mainstream legal scholars like me. It isn't that we have failed to explain the Constitution; it's that we too seldom try. Some scholars from top schools hold forth with polysyllabic theories of hermeneutics, or earnest invocations of Jürgen Habermas and Jacques Derrida, that ordinary citizens can't fathom. It's brilliant stuff; I like reading it. And it's the surest route to academic distinction. As a result, many of the most brilliant just don't try to speak outside the academic ghetto. Scholars who write for a popular audience often bear an invisible mark of shame, as if we were not quite full-fledged professors.

In addition, some progressive scholars feel shame-faced about defending the Constitution. Our country has a complex and sometimes problematic history. The Constitution as written reflected many past injustices. How can we reconcile that history with a commitment to the Constitution?

Conservatives have an easy response to these historical problems: they deny they exist. They claim that the "Founding Fathers" (a term coined by, of all people, Warren G. Harding[20]) were infallible, that neither the Constitution nor American history contain any mistakes. Michele Bachmann insisted that the Founding Fathers were really trying to abolish slavery when they wrote the Constitution. When challenged on that allegation, the best she could do was to cite John Quincy Adams, who was a twenty-year-old Harvard student when the Convention met, never set foot in Philadelphia that summer, and only became an abolitionist after he left the presidency in 1829. But to her, it was inconceivable that the "Founding Fathers" could really have been wrong, or short-sighted, or too self-interested to see the injustice of slavery.

Progressive critics of the Constitution say that it was written in 1787 by rich white men, many of them slaveholders, to protect their own racial, sexual, and economic privilege. The only answer to that charge is this: True enough. But we don't live under the Constitution set up in 1787. Over 225 years, the Constitution has been amended twenty-seven times. The first ten, of course, are the Bill of Rights, which restrain the federal government (and now the states) from violating individual rights. But many amendments after that have been designed to push American government and society in a progressive direction. The Thirteenth Amendment outlaws slavery in sweeping terms; the Fourteenth protects the civil rights and legal equality of citizens; the Fifteenth, Seventeenth, Twenty-Fourth, and Twenty-Sixth Amendments all expand the right to vote and protect it against state interference. The Sixteenth Amendment gives the federal government the power to enact a progressive income tax; the Seventeenth requires that the people, not legislators, choose United States senators.

The arrow of these amendments pushes one way—toward greater equality, greater democratic participation, and more effective power for the national government. Only one amendment ever passed has *limited* individual rights—the Eighteenth, which imposed Prohibition—and it was quickly repealed by the Twenty-First. The Constitution may have begun as a charter of privilege, but over the years, we the people have remade it into a document that, for all its flaws, embodies the progressive ideas of freedom, equality, national power, and self-government.

The Constitution—today's Constitution—belongs to all of us, and we should be glad to have it. It is the product of a long difficult, painful history, but it is no longer the flawed document written in 1787. It's time to take it back from those who are trying to steal it in plain sight. If we don't, the next time we need government—in the wake of a national disaster or a terrorist attack—we may find it has been dismantled. Our democratic Humpty Dumpty has been 225 years in the making; if we let the wrecking crew break him, he may be hard to put back together.

That's the reason for this book. While the Right has been spreading its myths, those who know better have been silent. I've been a constitutional scholar for twenty years. During the year before my trip to right-wing "Constitution school," I had spent almost every day reading and rereading the Constitution for a scholarly study of its text—a study I still hope to publish someday.

But I realized in that church basement that we need a book like this one more than another university-press study. Walk into any bookstore anywhere in America, and you'll find titles like *Who Killed the Constitution?*; *The Politically Incorrect™ Guide to the Constitution*; *Nullification: How to Resist Federal Tyranny in the 21st Century*; *What Would the Founders Say?*; or *The Constitution in Exile*—all expounding the Far Right's seductive, simplistic, and hateful message. On the other side of the ideological divide, we have either long, earnest guides to the Constitution or, well, nothing.

There's a need for ordinary people to push back against the far-right assault on the Constitution—the drive to destroy the Constitution in the name of "saving" it. So I resolved to write something that nonlawyers could use to pick apart the claims of the mystics and charlatans. To that end, I began to read far-right books, articles, and speeches, and I noticed that certain claims—claims that are demonstrably false—come up over and over. I began to make notes about them, and eventually I assembled a "top ten" list of falsehoods about the Constitution. The next section of this book is designed to provide the background information citizens need to understand that, no matter how emphatically these myths are shouted from the radio or the Internet, they are simply not true.

Here's a quick look at the claims we will discuss.

1. *Some people believe only in "original intent" and others believe in a "living Constitution."* Conservatives claim that they know and follow the real "intention" or "meaning" of the Constitution, while progressive and even moderate justices (even, sometimes, conservative Republican Justice Anthony Kennedy) merely consult their personal views and then pretend to "find" them in the Constitution. It's a phony argument. As we will see, progressive constitutional thinkers now and throughout American history have tried to apply the Constitution as it was written, intended, and understood. Conservative claims to know the "original intent" or "original public meaning" of the Constitution are in essence a power play to establish the Right alone as the arbiter of the Constitution's meaning.

2. *The Founders wrote the Constitution to restrain Congress and limit its powers.* Conservatives also claim that the Constitution was set up to restrain the federal government. The Philadelphia framers, they say, were terrified of federal power and created walls to hold it back. This view of the Constitution is more or less made out of whole cloth. The Constitution was set up to create a strong, effective government. Subsequent amendments have strengthened, not weakened, that structure. Most of the framers in Philadelphia were actually terrified of the short-sightedness and parochialism of the *states*, and wanted a federal government strong enough to keep them from pulling the new nation apart.

3. *Congress has distorted the meaning of the Commerce Power and used it to pass patently unconstitutional laws.* If there's one part of the Constitution that the Right hates, it's the Commerce Power. They claim that Congress's power over "commerce with foreign nations, and among the several states, and with the Indian tribes" has been "stretched" over the past century to cover things that have nothing to do with commerce. To support this claim, they have to distort both the history of the Constitution and the meaning of words. The Commerce Power was the centerpiece of the Philadelphia Constitution, and is needed if the United States is to remain a modern, first-world economy. Earlier judicial attempts to constrict it were disastrous. And the Right's real objection to contemporary Commerce Power doctrine is that it enables Congress to regulate . . . commerce.

4. *The Constitution does not provide for separation of church and state.* This idea, too, is far-right dogma. In their telling, "separation" was an invention of one man, Thomas Jefferson, and has nothing to do with

the "original intent" of the Constitution and the First Amendment. They claim that the Founders actually wanted the state governments to involve themselves in the spiritual lives of the people, guiding and directing them in proper belief—even, possibly, establishing one religious denomination, or Christianity generally, as the official state religion. The federal government, meanwhile, was to support all Christian religions equally, while disadvantaging all others. As we will see, this is dangerous nonsense. Separation is an American idea that long predates Jefferson. It was clearly embodied in the First Amendment, then incorporated in the Fourteenth Amendment. It applies to the states as much as to the federal government. It is a key to our continued unity and success as a nation.

5. *Equality and self-government are "wholly foreign to the First Amendment."* Why do we have freedom of speech? Is it a building block for a free self-governing republic, or a special tool of social control for consolidated wealth? Since 1974, the Right has begun to insist that free speech is a kind of asset, a form of wealth. For that reason, they say, rich people, institutions, and corporations are entitled to dominate national discourse and drown out anyone who has less money. After the Court's 2009 decision in *Citizens United v. Federal Election Commission*, this has begun to transform American politics, cementing domination of the process by rich individuals and institutions. Reasonable efforts to make sure all voices are heard, the Right increasingly says, are automatically unconstitutional. The only purpose of the First Amendment is to allow the rich to dominate discourse. That idea is wrong, and it's dangerous.

6. *The Second Amendment was "intended" to make government "fear the people."* The Far Right now has a goal: complete abolition of any regulation or licensing of firearms, either by the federal government or the states. They claim that the "intent" of the Second Amendment was to equip ordinary citizens to intimidate and resist government power. This idea is of very recent vintage. The extent of gun rights has been a subject for discussion for more than a century, but no reputable thinker ever suggested that the Second Amendment was there to let disgruntled citizens shoot down government officials when they feel like it. In fact, the history of the early republic suggests that the Founders took the possibility of armed resistance to government very seriously—and wanted it suppressed. The extremists who took over gun-owner groups

in the 1970s have a different agenda. Their view of civic life is of a constant war of all against all; as they push to make guns legal in bars, schools, airplanes, and churches, their vision poses a dire threat to the future of our society.

7. *The Tenth Amendment and state "sovereignty" allow states to "nullify" federal law.* The idea of "nullification" of federal law by state legislatures, as I said before, really stems from the racist resistance to the civil rights movement of the 1950s and 1960s. But today's radical Right likes to claim that the right to "nullify" federal law stems from the Tenth Amendment. They claim that the amendment "gives" states "rights" to resist federal "tyranny" and to protect their "sovereignty" against the federal government. But the idea that states have "rights," or that they are "sovereign" against the federal government, appears nowhere in the original Constitution. The Tenth Amendment certainly doesn't mention any of these concepts either; they were actually enshrined in the Articles of Confederation. The Articles were the first American "constitution"; they were discarded in 1787 largely because they gave the states too much control over national matters. Conservatives like to insert words into the Tenth Amendment when no one is looking; by doing so, they are distorting history and undermining the entire structure of the Constitution.

8. *The Fourteenth Amendment was written solely to address the situation of freed slaves, and has no relevance today.* The Fourteenth Amendment, with its guarantees of due process and equal protection, is probably the most important single amendment to the Constitution. Its framers, for the first time in American history, wrote into the Constitution's text the principle—originally stated in the Declaration of Independence— that human beings are created equal. Because it imposes the Bill of Rights on the state governments, it is the key to our democratic system. In areas from immigration to criminal justice to freedom of religion, its guarantees are ones we rely on every day. Enemies of equality have always hated it. The Right now claims that the Fourteenth Amendment really doesn't mean much. It was passed to protect freed slaves, they say; since there aren't any around today, it's a dead letter. Thus it doesn't provide any protection against sex discrimination, for example, or require states to observe the prohibition against established churches. The assault on the Fourteenth Amendment is a falsehood that endangers our basic freedoms and our right to self-government.

9. *Election of senators is unfair and harmful to the states.* The Right hates
the Seventeenth Amendment, which states that the members of the
Senate must be "elected by the people." They would like to return to
a system where the state legislative majority picked senators without
any messy popular vote. They claim this system was cleaner than the
current one; in fact, history shows precisely the opposite to be true.
They also claim that popular election of senators has destroyed "states'
rights." That claim, too, is demonstrably untrue. Like members of the
House, senators continue to represent their states. Members of Congress help carry on the constant political bargaining between states
and the federal government. What the Right hates about popular
election is that it prevents state legislators from interfering directly in
Congress. Instead, senators are responsible to those idiots, the voters.
10. *International law is a threat to the Constitution and must be kept out
of American courts.* Like Justice of the Peace Pearce, who taught my
"Constitution school," the Far Right professes to be terrified that the
insidious force of international law is reducing the United States from
an independent nation to a servile satrapy of the United Nations—or,
even worse, a province of the imagined Islamic Caliphate spreading
across the globe. The idea that "Sharia law" is slowly taking control
of our communities is ridiculous. Those who spread it are serving a
destructive agenda of religious hatred. The larger idea behind this
myth is that the United States can declare itself free of any obligations to other countries. In this version, the Constitution is supposed
to exempt the United States from its role in the world system. That
idea has no basis in history. It could undermine our entire economic
system and even endanger the peace. The framers of the Constitution
knew this, which is why they explicitly wrote into the Constitution a
requirement that courts *must* consider international law.

Most of these claims—like the nonsense about the anti-federal "purpose" of the Constitution or the "true meaning" of the Tenth Amendment—are refuted simply by a careful reading of the Constitution's text.
What's remarkable is how few people actually do this before proclaiming
their opinions. Even most lawyers have never read the document straight
through: in most law schools, constitutional law courses don't even begin
with the text. A lot of self-proclaimed experts on the Constitution don't
seem to have read it either. Herman Cain, for example, excoriated liberals

for not knowing that the Constitution said "it is the right of the people to alter or abolish" government.[21] Cain was quoting the Declaration of Independence, which was written in 1776, not 1787, and is not the supreme law of the land.

The text of the Constitution is printed at the back of this book. As you go through the book, read the text and measure it against the absurd claims we hear every day. I think you'll be struck by one fact: the "policies" the Right claims to find in the Constitution—whether they are libertarian economics or Christian government—aren't there.

This book is designed to arm readers with the ammunition they need to combat mythology and deception wherever they encounter it. The Right is trying to steal the Constitution in plain sight. If we don't challenge the nonsense being spread about our form of government, we will find that it has been changed into something unrecognizable.

Ordinary Americans love the Constitution at least as much as far-right ideologues. It's our Constitution, too.

Before it's too late, we need to take it back.

THE TEN BIG MYTHS

CHAPTER 1

The Right Is "Originalist"; Everyone Else Is "Idiotic"

In a 2006 speech in Puerto Rico, Justice Antonin Scalia explained that only conservatives actually believe in the Constitution. Progressives, he said, believe in "the argument of flexibility," which "goes something like this: The Constitution is over 200 years old and societies change. It has to change with society, like a living organism, or it will become brittle and break. But you would have to be an idiot to believe that. The Constitution is not a living organism, it is a legal document. It says something, and doesn't say other things."[1]

A year later, President George W. Bush told the Federalist Society, "Advocates of a more active role for judges sometimes talk of a 'living constitution.' In practice, a living Constitution means whatever these activists want it to mean."[2]

Originalism, writes scholar David Forte in *The Heritage Guide to the Constitution*, "implies that those who make, interpret, and enforce the law ought to be guided by the meaning of the U.S. Constitution—the supreme law of the land—as it was originally written." Who could be against that? Nobody, Forte writes, except those who believe that the Constitution has "no fixed meaning."[3]

The Right's invented definition of a "living constitution" is useful because it lets right-wingers like Scalia pose as principled advocates and ridicule anyone who disagrees with his narrow ideas. Note that the idea is that the Constitution "says something, and doesn't say other things"—in other words, those who don't read it the way Scalia does must believe it says nothing at all.

In fact, the argument is a classic bait-and-switch. It begins with the claim that every part of the Constitution when adopted had a fixed, precise meaning. We must apply that meaning and only that meaning, or we are "changing" the Constitution. As Scalia said, everyone else is an idiot who makes it up—an unpatriotic elite deceiver.

"Fixed meaning" is the snapper here. Very often, the words themselves aren't clear. (What, for example, is "due process of law," or "cruel and unusual punishment," or "unreasonable seizure"?) Then the Right explains that their *meaning* isn't what's written in the Constitution's text; it is actually somewhere else. The words on the page have to be interpreted in a secret way that conservatives "know" because they have looked it up in the Big History Book. That's true, as we'll see, even when the non-originalist is suggesting that the words mean what they literally say. If we do not accept the Right's claims about what the words "really" mean, we are "changing" what is written on the page, trying to "amend" it on the sly.

The popular myth of "original intent" rests on the notion that there is somehow a single "clear" intent hidden in each phrase of the Constitution. (The phrase "clear intent," by the way, ought to serve as warning that an attempt to pick your pocket is in progress.) That idea confuses the task of reading the Constitution with the work of a Protestant believer reading the Bible. Religious historian Jaroslav Pelikan sees the origins of American constitutional discourse in early Protestant theology. Luther and the other Reformers believed that "Scripture had to be not interpreted but delivered from interpretations to speak for itself," Pelikan writes. What mattered to Luther was "the original intent and *sensus literalis* [literal meaning]" of the words of the Bible."[4]

A century ago, a group of American evangelical Christians published a set of essays on their Christian beliefs that was later published in book form as *The Fundamentals*. In large part, what came to be called "fundamentalism" was a revolt against nineteenth-century "higher criticism"— scholarship that studied the Bible like any other literary or historical text. Rejecting this approach, fundamentalists argued that the Bible is the literal word of God; all parts of it are created directly by inspiration, the breath of God into the human soul. Not only the ideas but also the very words in which they were written flow directly from God. "The Bible is made up of writings, and these are composed of words. The words are inspired— God-breathed. Therefore is the Bible inspired—*is* God's Word."[5]

Every word has an eternal meaning; all the words fit together into one divine whole. This "true" meaning, available only to the faithful, must be zealously guarded against corrupt worldly forces—the "higher critics"— seeking to contaminate it with modern, un-Christian ideas. "The higher criticism has been in the hands of men who disavow belief in God and Jesus Christ," one *Fundamentals* author explained. "Therefore their theory is truly a revolutionary one."[6]

"Originalist" political figures and talking heads have taken—sometimes without knowing it—their basic ideas straight from the fundamentalist canon. They treat the Constitution the way many fundamentalist Christians treat the Bible—as an infallible, inerrant, consistent, timeless document. In fact, the biblical view of the Constitution gives to our fundamental law a kind of scriptural shape. We have the Law (the 1787 Constitution) writ-ten by the Patriarchs (the "Founding Fathers"). We have (as Pelikan notes) the Ten Commandments (the Bill of Rights). And we even have a set of Epistles—*The Federalist*, written after the Constitutional Convention by James Madison (who was present every day of the Convention), Alexander Hamilton (who was a delegate but rarely attended), and John Jay (who wasn't a delegate at all). These essays were written in haste in an effort to convince the voters of New York to back the new Constitution; often, as Pauline Maier notes in her history of the ratification of the Constitution, the authors did not have time to show them to each other. And they had relatively little to do with ratification except in some parts of New York.[7]

The Far Right, however, now insists these essays are divine writ. An-thony A. Peacock of Utah State University, writing in a Heritage Founda-tion pamphlet, treats the multiple authorship of *The Federalist* in almost the precise language that a fundamentalist would use for dealing with the multiple authors of the Bible: "Use of a single pseudonym suggested that *The Federalist* possessed a uniformity of intent: that *The Federalist* was to be read as the work of one mind, not three, and was coherent through-out."[8] Peacock adds, again in language that could have appeared in *The Fundamentals*, "The teaching of *The Federalist* was intended to be true for all times and all places."[9]

The analogy goes further: "originalists" have an enemy just as the fundamentalists did. The "higher critics," to fundamentalists, were devious elites who misunderstood and misrepresented the Bible because they were not true Christians. In much the same way, the supposed advocates of the "living Constitution" are smooth-talking, anti-American "elite" deceivers who want to replace the good old Constitution with their personal, foreign-influenced views.

But that's one of the Right's biggest lies. "We are all federalists, we are all republicans," Thomas Jefferson said in his first inaugural address. And we are all "originalists." Many constitutional interpreters like me, however, find the "original intent," or "original meaning," in, well, what the Constitution says. The only thing we know for sure that all the Founders "intended" was *to write the words of the Constitution*. Any principled interpretation has to start there.

And there's at least one wrong way to read the words—and that's to read them as if they were Bible verses. Whatever your faith about scripture, a moment's thought will convince you that the Constitution can't be Holy Writ. Indeed, the very idea is faintly blasphemous. The men who wrote the Constitution were smart and public spirited, but they were also—as they knew themselves—fallible and far from all-knowing. They were working under great pressure, dealing with an immediate political situation that was changing day to day. There was no burning bush, no voice from the whirlwind, no tablet of stone. The process involved human beings improvising something new: the first *written* constitution for an entire nation. They had very little clear sense of what would happen to America in the two decades after they wrote—much less in the two centuries after that. We can only read their words as a human product, with all the contradictions, vagueness, and gaps that implies.

We read it, then, as a practical document, to be applied to unforeseen circumstances. If the Constitution says that Congress has the power to regulate "commerce with foreign nations, and among the several states, and with the Indian tribes," we look around us and ask what areas of today's national life are part of "commerce." If the eighteenth century's village "barber chirurgeon" has been replaced by a nationwide for-profit hospital chain and a private system of group health insurance, then the power of Congress tracks that change. That's an act of interpretation, to be sure, but it's no more of one than the charade engaged in by many far-right "originalists."

For all their claims of superior virtue, "originalists" agree that what the Founders said governs; they just want to control what counts as what the Founders said. At their baldest and strongest, originalists claim that the nation is bound by *their own opinion* of what was in the minds of the framers or of those who ratified.

My quarrel is not with serious legal scholars and historians. Serious originalist scholarship is very useful as one way of learning more about the Constitution. Reputable originalist scholars rarely claim to *know* what was in the mind of the American people in 1787. In that sense, I am an originalist and frequently attend conferences on "originalism." It is always worthwhile to write about the intellectual and political world of the framers of the various parts of the Constitution. But that is only one part of any serious inquiry into how a constitutional provision applies to a present situation.

Real historians are quite modest about their ability to pin down complex questions of intellectual history with certainty. What they do say, correctly, is that we can learn much about the growth of American government by studying what members of the founding generation said about what they expected the Constitution to achieve. This study is very valuable—and there is no question that it can shed light on contemporary constitutional questions.

But in the hands of right-wing judges and demagogues, genuine originalism morphs into "originalism"—a kind of intellectual weapon designed to hide from ordinary citizens what is in plain sight—the text of the Constitution and the present circumstances to which it must be applied.

In fact, far-right "originalism" actually comprises a variety of techniques designed to eclipse the text and history of the Constitution and impose a specific meaning on each provision—a meaning that by coincidence usually matches the political program of the twenty-first-century Right. Here's a guide to those techniques, which we will refer back to later in this book.

1. *"Everybody Knows" Originalism.* In this version, an originalist can simply import ideas into the text that aren't referenced there, or in the specific history of that text's adoption. This is done by saying that "everybody knows" what the framers really thought about a given subject, and thus that the words on the page *couldn't* mean what they seem to say. This method of originalism appears in the most disastrous Supreme Court opinion ever written, Chief Justice Roger B. Taney's majority opinion in *Dred Scott.* In that opinion, Taney, a former slaveholder, discovered that persons of African descent, even if born in the United States, were not U.S. citizens and never could become U.S.

citizens, even if Congress used its naturalization power to make them so. There's nothing in the text restricting citizenship by race. But, to Taney, *everybody knew* that the framers regarded black Americans, slave or free, as "far below them in the scale of created beings,"[10] and thus could not have intended to allow them to have citizenship. They just somehow forgot to say so.

Dred Scott is widely rejected now, but "everybody knows" originalism lives on. It was on display in Justice Clarence Thomas's dissent in *Brown v. Entertainment Merchants Association*, in which the Supreme Court majority held that the First Amendment did not allow California to make it a crime to sell a violent video game to a minor. This was fairly straightforward free-speech doctrine—but Thomas indignantly dissented because, though he had no case law to support him, "everybody knows" that people in the eighteenth century didn't believe that adults had any right to talk to children who didn't belong to them: "The historical evidence shows that the founding generation believed parents had absolute authority over their minor children and expected parents to use that authority to direct the proper development of their children. It would be absurd to suggest that such a society understood 'the freedom of speech' to include a right to speak to minors (or a corresponding right of minors to access speech) without going through the minors' parents."[11] We know they must have thought that; therefore, let's pretend they said that.

2. *Da Vinci Code Originalism.* In this mode of interpretation, conservative interpreters simply wipe out the words of the Constitution themselves and insist that they are a secret reference to other words. A good example of this is the way that anti-immigration politicians are now "interpreting" the Citizenship Clause of the Fourteenth Amendment. That clause, the first in the amendment, says, "All persons born or naturalized in the United States, and subject to the jurisdiction thereof, are citizens of the United States and of the State wherein they reside."

These words aren't hard to understand and apply. If a child is born inside the United States, and has no special legal status—diplomatic immunity from U.S. law—then the child is a citizen. The problem with that is it's inconvenient for the extremists who want to strip citizenship from American-born children of undocumented aliens. So they have simply begun saying that "subject to the jurisdiction" means something different from what it says—"not having any relationship, even through parents, to any foreign country." This interpretation is fairly recent—even W. Cleon Skousen, writing in 1985, doesn't refer to it—because the Da Vinci Code "originalists" have invented it to fill a present political need.

3. *"Voices in the Head" Originalism.* In this version, the interpreter confronts evidence that some members—perhaps most—of the founding generation did, in fact, *not* interpret the Constitution in the way the right wing now needs it to be interpreted. That problem is easily overcome—the interpreter simply explains that he knows that if the Founders had known then what *he* knows now, they would agree with him.

Justice Scalia himself is a proud practitioner of this dark art. It's on display in his concurrence in the 2009 case of *Citizens United v. Federal Elections Commission*, which held that the First Amendment bars any restrictions on independent campaign expenditures by profit-making corporations. Justice John Paul Stevens, in his dissent, had questioned the majority's radical ruling on "originalist" grounds. Private corporations were relatively new at the time of the framing of the First Amendment, Stevens noted, and many of the framers were profoundly suspicious of the corporate form. Can we say that they "intended" Chevron to be able to flood the political process with electioneering messages?

Scalia brushed this aside. The framers opposed corporations because they incorrectly associated them with monopoly, Scalia explained. "Modern corporations do not have such privileges, and would probably have been favored by most of our enterprising Founders—excluding, perhaps, Thomas Jefferson and others favoring perpetuation of an agrarian society."[12]

In other words, trust me, I knew the Founders, I worked with the Founders, the Founders were friends of mine. The "original meaning" is what I say the Founders would say if they were alive today.

4. *"Pay No Attention to That Man Behind the Curtain" Originalism.* This is another counter to evidence that one or more of the framers or ratifiers of the Constitution did not agree with a position urged by the Far Right. If the evidence is strong, you simply deny that this particular framer is particularly important. Poor James Madison—perhaps the main intellectual author of the Constitution, one of the cowriters of *The Federalist*, and the main sponsor of the Bill of Rights—is often shuffled off stage this way. Madison's view of church and state is very

inconvenient for the Far Right, because he sternly believed that religion had no place in government at any level, and that politicians should neither subsidize churches nor even make use of religion in their public pronouncements.

David Barton, the phony "historian" so beloved of the Christian right, explains it this way: Madison may have opposed government support of religion, but "Madison—while undeniably an important influence during the Constitutional Convention—was often out of step with the majority of the delegates."[13]

In his opinion in *Rosenberger v. Rector and Visitors of the University of Virginia*, Justice Thomas was confronted by Justice Souter, who quoted Madison in adamant opposition to the idea of government subsidy to religious organizations. In *Rosenberger*, however, the majority had decided that a public university could not refuse student-fee subsidies to a student newspaper founded to convince young people to accept Jesus.

Madison's views are inconvenient for the current right-wing project of imposing religious observance on the nation; in response, Justice Thomas wrote, "even if more extreme notions of the separation of church and state can be attributed to Madison, the views of one man do not establish the original understanding of the First Amendment."[14] The Founders may be all very well—until they disagree with today's Far Right, at which point they become extremists.

5. *"Foresight" Originalism.* If all else fails, the Right abandons the idea of an original "intent" or "meaning" and simply says that a given idea must be unconstitutional because the Founders would never have foreseen it. The worst insult they can level at a governmental measure is that it is "unprecedented." Before the Civil War, conservatives argued that Congress couldn't build roads and canals; it was unprecedented. After the Civil War, Congress "couldn't" regulate child labor; it was unprecedented. When the Depression hit, Congress "couldn't" pass Social Security; it was unprecedented. When the civil rights movement arose, Congress "couldn't" outlaw discrimination in public accommodations; it was unprecedented. Medicare was unprecedented; so was the National Environmental Policy Act; so was the school lunch program. Today, Congress "can't" enact a health care system. We've never had one, so we can't have one.

Remember the confusion some conservatives have between the Founders and the prophets of ancient Israel? They truly imagine that the fifty-five men who gathered at Philadelphia were foreseeing a world of atomic weapons, aviation, instantaneous communication, the Internet, credit cards, and Monday Night Football. That idea, brought out into the light of day, is ludicrous. The framers didn't know what would happen next, and they wanted a government that could handle whatever comes up. The Constitution itself did the unprecedented. It created a national, republican government with adequate power to maintain and govern a strong Union during the unforeseeable events ahead. Contemporary interpretation should respect *that* "intention," rather than inventing claims about what they foresaw. "Nothing can therefore be more fallacious, than to infer the extent of any power, proper to be lodged in the National Government, from an estimate of its immediate necessities," Alexander Hamilton wrote in *The Federalist*. "There ought to be a capacity to provide for future contingencies, as they may happen; and, as these are illimitable in their nature, it is impossible safely to limit that capacity."[15]

If you don't believe me and Hamilton, consider these words from a conservative icon, former chief justice William H. Rehnquist: "Merely because a particular activity may not have existed when the Constitution was adopted, or because the framers could not have conceived of a particular method of transacting affairs, cannot mean that general language in the Constitution may not be applied to such a course of conduct. Where the framers of the Constitution have used general language, they have given latitude to those who would later interpret the instrument to make that language applicable to cases that the framers might not have foreseen."[16]

This catalog of the distortions caused by sloppy "originalism" ought to make it clear that the Right's attack on the "living Constitution" label is about as useful as a Tannu Tuva stamp. All conscientious judges, of whatever philosophy, are trying to apply the words of the Constitution. But almost no serious constitutional question involves precise, unambiguous words. The Constitution says that the president has to be thirty-five years old, for example; no one I am aware of has ever challenged that rule by arguing that since fifty is the new thirty, the president should now have to be at least fifty-five. The Third Amendment prohibits quartering of troops in private homes in time of peace—an easy rule to follow, and one that has almost never given rise to a dispute.

Instead, genuine constitutional controversies center around general terms used in the document. Take one that has been prominent lately—"natural-born citizen." The Constitution doesn't define the term. In 2008, one major-party candidate, it seemed, might not fit that description. It wasn't Barack Obama, who was born in Hawaii; it was Senator John McCain, who was born in the Panama Canal Zone, where his father was stationed on naval duty. The zone was Panamanian territory; however, by treaty between Panama and the United States, it was property of the Panama Canal Company. The head of the company was governor of the zone. U.S. law applied to those who lived in its territory.

One legal scholar suggested in a law review article that, under the law as it was at McCain's birth, he did not qualify as a "natural-born citizen."[17] Other scholars disagreed. There was no Big History Book to answer that question. So, in April 2008, the Senate passed a bipartisan resolution stating that McCain was a "natural-born citizen" and thus eligible to be president.

An "originalist" inquiry into this question would have been worse than useless. Remember that in 1787 there were no U.S. military personnel serving abroad; indeed, many of the framers assumed there never would be a standing army, and that a self-governing republic would eschew foreign conquest and occupation. (No U.S. troops were sent on foreign occupation duty until the Mexican War of 1846–1848.) So did they "intend" or "understand" the "natural-born citizen" clause to apply to children of troops stationed in foreign territory under U.S. sovereignty or not? The evidence either way is nonexistent.

One of the measure's sponsors was Senator Tom Coburn (R-OK), one of the Senate's loudest "originalists." Was Coburn being a hypocritical "living constitutionalist" then? Certainly not. He was being a *good* constitutionalist—not an "originalist," not a "living constitutionalist"—applying an unclear term to a new and unforeseen circumstance.

Americans of all stripes do exactly this every day with terms like "due process" or "commerce . . . among the several states." Like "natural-born citizen," those terms were ambiguous when written, and they are ambiguous today. There's no evidence that the framers had a Really Big Book of Definitions with the complete "intended" meaning of any of them in it. The job of constitutional interpretation is to apply these ambiguous general terms to the changing facts of American government and society. Does attaching a GPS to a citizen's car violate the Fourth Amendment's prohibition against "unreasonable searches"? What about a strip-search for persons arrested for traffic offenses, or a full-body scan at airports?

Are individual decisions about how to pay for health care and health insurance "commerce . . . among the several states"? The framers wouldn't have said "yes" or "no"; they would have said, "What is health insurance?"

If you think that answer means that "commerce" today doesn't extend to health insurance, you aren't supporting a "living Constitution"—you are describing a dead society whose fundamental law cannot be applied to the facts of our national life.

When they are in favor of warrantless wiretaps or "enemy-combatant" detentions, many conservatives like to explain that the Constitution is not a suicide pact. Maybe not. But it's not a killing jar either, designed to freeze society in an eighteenth-century mold. The most important truth about the Constitution is this: it was written as a set of rules by which living people could solve their own problems, not as a "dead hand" restricting their options. Strikingly, many important questions, from the size of the Supreme Court to the line of presidential succession, are left to Congress. The framers didn't think of themselves as peering into the future and settling all questions; instead, they wrote a document that in essence says, "Work it out." It is a set of general rules that we, the living, must apply, in a fully textual sense, to unforeseen specific cases.

I will cheerfully admit that conscientious conservative judges and scholars may differ with me on the specific application of a given provision. My hat's off to them. The Constitution was written to give us something to argue about, and most of these important issues are also hard ones.

But in reaching their conclusions, conservatives rely on the same tools progressives do—text, structure, history, political philosophy, interpretive theory, and practicality. When Justice Scalia—or anyone else in this context—describes those who differ with him as idiots, he is not just being rude and vulgar—he is also being dishonest.

CHAPTER 2

The "Purpose" of the Constitution Is to Limit Congress

"The Constitution was written explicitly for one purpose—to restrain the federal government," Representative Ron Paul said in 2008.[1]

Bless his heart. (For those of you who didn't grow up in the South, that expression in context means, "Sometimes I just want to slap him.") Dr. Paul knows as much about the Constitution as I do about obstetrics—the difference being that I don't try to instruct the nation on how to deliver babies.

Dr. Paul is far from alone in this bizarre delusion. If there's anything the Far Right regards as dogma, it's that the "intent" of the Constitution was to restrain, inhibit, intimidate, infantilize, disempower, disembowel, and generally smack the federal government around. "Does anyone seriously believe that when the Founders gathered in Philadelphia 220 years ago they were aspiring to control the buying decisions of individual consumers from Washington?" Senator Tom Coburn asks. "They were arguing for the opposite and implored future Courts to slap down any law from Congress that expanded the Commerce Clause."[2] Senator Jim DeMint calls our founding charter "the Constitution of No,"[3] and argues that "although the Constitution does give some defined powers to the federal government, it is overwhelmingly a document of limits, and those limits must be respected."[4]

If this is true, it's the kind of truth that comes from voices in DeMint's head—because it sure doesn't appear in the text of the Constitution, the history of its framing, or the debate in the new nation after the Constitution was proposed. (Note Dr. Paul's use of the word "explicitly" above. He is using it the way many people use "literally" in ordinary speech today. What he means is "*not* explicitly," but that doesn't sound as convincing.)

Historically, in fact, the idea that the framers wanted to stymie a powerful government, that they feared Congress or federal power generally, is ludicrously anachronistic, like claiming that the telescope was invented in 1608 so that people could watch Apollo 11 land on the moon.

There was no federal government to speak of in 1787. The entire government had fewer workers than George Washington's Mount Vernon plantation. "Congress" was a feckless, ludicrous farce. The concern that brought delegates to Philadelphia was that, under the Articles of Confederation, Congress was too weak.

Consider how the Articles worked: They weren't actually a national constitution, but a "firm league of friendship" between independent mininations. Each state appointed any number of delegates to Congress—it didn't matter how many because each state had one vote no matter what. States had to pay the salaries of their members of Congress, and could recall their members at any time. Congress could not make any significant decision without the votes of nine states. States could, and often did, just not bother to send delegates, which saved them money and also made it less likely that Congress would do anything annoying.

Congress was to pay the costs of war and other national expenses, but to get the money it had to request each state to impose taxes on its people, generating sums "in proportion to the value of all land within each state."[5]

There were no federal courts. There was no president or executive branch. If Congress adjourned, it could—but was not required to—appoint a committee of members to make emergency decisions whenever it was not in session. But nine states had to agree on any such decision.

Congress was to direct American forces in time of war—but to assemble them, it had to request each state to muster its militia and send them to national service. No matter how grave the threat, each state was responsible only for a share of the total number of troops needed "in proportion to the number of white inhabitants in such State." Each state was supposed to provide all the arms and supplies for its militia. What could Congress do if a state refused to send the money Congress asked for, or raise the troops it needed, or comply with an international treaty Congress had approved? Nothing.

Look at Washington, D.C., today, and ask yourself what the nation could achieve if members of Congress didn't need to show up, if a supermajority was needed for any measure, if state legislatures were expected to collect federal taxes, if no federal courts existed to enforce federal law, and if there were no president. The answer again is, in a word, nothing.

That powerless government drove the framers close to panic. The Confederation Congress was unable to levy taxes, pay the nation's debts, live up to its treaty obligations, regulate commerce, or restrain the predatory state governments. In particular, the states refused to comply with the Treaty of Paris that ended the Revolutionary War. If state citizens owed Britons money, Article IV of the treaty obligated the states to enforce the debts. Under Article V, states were expected to return all property confiscated from Englishmen and loyalists during the war. The states refused to comply with either requirement, and the British used this as an excuse to maintain military forces in the West, encroaching on land the treaty had given to the United States.

Meanwhile, the states themselves engaged in trade wars among themselves, taxing out-of-state goods—or embargoing them altogether—in ways that disrupted the growth of a national market. The Union was surrounded by two of the most powerful empires in the world: Britain and Spain. The third, France, was angling for a foothold in North America as well. The American government, however, was terminally weak and disunited. The United States seemed on the verge of splitting into tiny republics, which would quickly become colonies of some European power.

As early as 1780, Alexander Hamilton (one of the authors of *The Federalist*) had written to James Duane that "[t]he fundamental defect [in the Articles of Confederation] is a want of power in Congress. It is hardly worth while to show in what this consists, as it seems to be universally acknowledged, or to point out how it has happened, as the only question is how to remedy it."[6]

George Washington agreed. As early as 1783, he was offering a toast at celebratory dinners: "Competent powers to congress for general purposes."[7] In 1784, he wrote to Benjamin Harrison, "The disinclination of the individual States to yield competent powers to Congress for the Fœderal Government—their unreasonable jealousy of that body & of one another—& the disposition which seems to pervade each, of being all-wise & all-powerful within itself, will, if there is not a change in the system, be our downfall as a Nation."[8]

In April 1787, James Madison (another author of *The Federalist*) wrote to Washington about his own hopes for a new Constitution: "The

national government should be armed with positive and compleat authority in all cases which require uniformity."[9] Madison wanted a rule that no
state law could take effect until Congress explicitly approved it. Earlier,
Washington had written to John Jay, "I do not conceive we can exist long
as a nation, without having lodged somewhere a power which will pervade
the whole Union in as energetic a manner, as the authority of the different
state governments extends over the several States."[10] Jay (third author of
The Federalist) agreed: "What Powers should be granted to the Government so constituted is a Question which deserves much Thought—I think
the more the better—the States retaining only so much as may be necessary for domestic Purposes; and all their principal Officers civil and military being commissioned and removeable by the national Governmt."[11]

The majority of delegates to the Philadelphia Convention agreed with
the future authors of The Federalist: the new Constitution must radically
strengthen Congress and create a full government to carry out its will. In
his opening speech, Virginia governor Edmund Randolph presented the
"Virginia plan," which became the basis of the Constitution. He warned
that under the Articles of Confederation, "the federal government could
not check the quarrels between states, nor a rebellion in any, not having
constitutional power nor means to interpose according to the exigency,"
and that the new nation faced "the prospect of anarchy from the laxity of
government everywhere."[12]

The Virginia plan originally proposed that Congress have the power
"to legislate in all cases to which the separate States are incompetent, or
in which the harmony of the United States may be interrupted by the
exercise of individual legislation; to negative all laws passed by the several
states, contravening in the opinion of the National Legislature the articles
of Union; and to call forth the force of the Union against any member of
the Union failing to fulfill its duty under the articles thereof."[13]

Compared to many in Philadelphia, however, Randolph was relatively
moderate on the issue of federal power. A number of other delegates
would have gone further. The federal veto on state laws was a project dear
to Madison's heart, and he gave it up only reluctantly as the Convention
progressed. Hamilton wanted the federal government to appoint the state
governors. Gouverneur Morris, one of the most influential delegates,
favored "a national, supreme, government . . . having a compleat and
compulsive operation."[14]

Of course, other delegates wanted a less active role for the federal government. Randolph himself refused to sign the document at the end of the Convention because he found the new government too powerful. But there's little question that the Constitution the Convention actually wrote created a strong federal government. The only serious question is about the degree of strength—not about an imaginary preference for weakness.

The Convention decided to enumerate the powers of Congress in Article I § 8. Some commentators have concluded the framers listed specific powers because the Convention had come to desire taking a narrow view of those powers, but if so, the text sure doesn't say so. Article I, which sets up and empowers Congress, is by far the longest and most detailed article in the document. Section 8, which lists the powers of Congress, is the heart of it.

Read the list of powers all at once: their scope is nearly breathtaking. It goes far beyond the feeble powers under the Articles. Congress was empowered to levy taxes directly on the people, to borrow and repay debts, and to regulate commerce "with foreign nations, and among the several states, and with the Indian tribes." Congress was given complete control of a national capital, which would belong to no state. It was given exclusive power to determine who could become a naturalized U.S. citizen. It alone could issue money and fix its value. It could grant limited monopolies to authors and inventors. It was required to create a Supreme Court and permitted to create an entire national court system. It could raise an army and a navy in time of war or peace, without so much as a "by your leave" to the states. In fact, Congress could take virtually complete control of the state militia at any time it chose, down to the power to use militia forces against recalcitrant or rebellious states.

To underline the power of Congress, the framers began the list of powers with a provision allowing Congress to impose taxes "to provide for the common defense and general welfare of the United States." It ended the list by adding the power "to make all laws which shall be necessary and proper for carrying into execution the foregoing powers, and all other powers vested by this Constitution in the government of the United States, or in any department or officer thereof."

The last words are significant. One thing the Far Right likes to do is insist that all federal power is contained in Article I § 8. As we've seen, even if that were true, the federal government, and Congress, would have a lot of power. But it's not true. Elsewhere in its text, the Constitution grants other sweeping powers to Congress.

Here are a few powers granted outside of Article I: Congress can impeach and remove the president and all federal officials and judges. It can regulate the time, place, and manner in which the states conduct federal elections, and the date of presidential elections. Each House can decide the winner of any election for one of its members. The two Houses together can, by supermajority, propose an amendment to the Constitution. Congress determines who succeeds to the presidency if neither the president nor vice president can serve. Congress creates the cabinet departments and sets their responsibilities. Congress creates the Supreme Court, sets the number of its justices, and regulates its jurisdiction. Congress decides whether to set up lower courts, and which ones there will be. It sets the punishment for treason and creates rules by which state acts can be proved in order to receive "full faith and credit." Congress has exclusive power over all U.S. territories. And it can admit new states whenever it wants. The federal courts have their own powers, explicit and implied, and so does the president, and the "necessary and proper" clause gives Congress power to carry those into effect as well.

If this is an "intent" to limit, it's hard to imagine what an intent to *empower* would look like. The document as a whole is much more concerned with what the government *can* do than with what it can't. To be sure, restrictions on Congress's power appear in Article I § 9. Congress can't grant titles of nobility. It can't shortcut the criminal justice system by passing "bills of attainder" or making conduct criminal after the fact. It can't tax exports, favor one state's seaports over those of another, or require ships bound for one state to clear customs in another. It can apparently suspend the writ of habeas corpus, but only when "in cases of rebellion or invasion the public safety may require it." However, the textual grants of power far overbalance the textual restrictions.

States, by contrast, were much more sharply limited; look at Article I § 10. They could not issue their own money, or negotiate with foreign countries, or even with each other unless Congress gave approval in advance. They could not maintain troops or navies. Elsewhere, the Constitution gave the federal government the power to "guarantee to every state in this union a republican form of government," meaning that state constitutions must meet federal approval. Federal courts were given power to settle disputes between states.

Chief Justice John Marshall, who took part in the Virginia ratifying convention, read the document and, in one of his most important opinions, laid out the powers he saw there: "we find the great powers, to lay and collect taxes; to borrow money; to regulate commerce; to declare and conduct a war; and to raise and support armies and navies. The sword and the purse, all the external relations, and no inconsiderable portion of the industry of the nation, are intrusted to its government."[15]

Right-wing constitutionalists don't reject this evidence; they evade it by changing the terms of the argument. To those who cite the full textual extent of federal and congressional power, they respond by accusing them of saying that there are *no* limits on the federal government's powers. For example, law professors Randy E. Barnett and Elizabeth Price Foley claim that applying the Necessary and Proper Clause as authorizing the Patient Protection and Affordable Care Act "would fundamentally transform our constitutional scheme from limited to unlimited federal power, narrowing the scope of individual liberty."[16] But that's palpably untrue.

As we will see, the Constitution's text sets out two kinds of limits on the national government. The first set concerns individual rights. The federal government can't throw people in jail without a good reason, or steal their property, or do away with free elections. The original Constitution prohibited a number of oppressive practices, like bills of attainder. The Bill of Rights added other restrictions.

The second set of restrictions, however, lies in the political structure of the Constitution. The framers' main plan for preventing overreach by the federal government lay not in coded restrictions on Congress's powers but in a system that would allow the people to limit government when they chose. This is what George Washington meant when he expressed hope that "a liberal, and energetic Constitution, well guarded & closely watched, to prevent incroachments, might restore us to that degree of respectability & consequence, to which we had a fair claim, & the brightest prospect of attaining."[17]

The idea was that a free political system, with roles for the people and for the states, would prevent the federal government from acting hastily or overreaching. To begin with, all laws had to pass both houses of Congress, which were independent of each other. Each member of either house represented a state, and could be expected to watch out for that state's interests. After they overcame that hurdle, proposed laws had to be signed by the president. This separation between legislative and executive power would channel Congress's broad powers into constructive channels. When Congress met, state governments—and citizens—would advocate effectively for their own interests both in Congress and with the president. They did that from the very beginning and they do that today. Finally, the people would have a say on what Congress had done—at the ballot box. Far from suggesting no limits on Congress's power, the PPACA and its aftermath make clear that this political structure actually works remarkably well. Health care is now a subject of general debate, and a major issue in the presidential election. Can anyone really argue that without courts to invent new non-textual limits, the people would be at Congress's mercy?

In this Constitution, the real one, there's no sign of the libertarian Never Never Land many on the far right believe in. Nor is there any trace of a nation where the states are supreme in any area. Rather, the Constitution allowed for a government adequate to the challenges facing a modern nation. It's not surprising: this document was written by delegates who feared that America faced a danger of division and foreign conquest. They wanted to make sure the new government could rise to any challenge. "It is both unwise and dangerous," Alexander Hamilton wrote in Federalist No. 23, "to deny the federal government an unconfined authority, as to all those objects which are intrusted to its management."[18] The safeguard against misuse of that power, he added, lay in popular elections, not in rigid ideological rules.

So from the beginning, the Constitution gave broad power to the federal government. Over time, we the people have given that government even more power to "promote the general welfare." As I noted in the introduction, each of the major amendments guaranteeing rights since 1864 has included a grant of power to Congress to enforce its provisions. All told, the Constitution gives the new government a lot of power. And over the years, the government has sometimes needed it to deal with civil war, economic calamity, natural disaster, and internal disorder. Our government, and its constitutional powers, is vital to our survival as a nation. These institutions are worthy of respect and defense.

The far-right argument has the seductive power of any half-truth. Of course there are limits on Congress's power—as we've seen, they are located in Article I § 9 and in the Bill of Rights. But by "limits," conservatives mean something different: What they mean is that if something isn't written down in the Constitution in so many words, the "intent" of the framers was that Congress could never do it. If Congress wasn't doing it before 1787, it can't do it now.

Contemporary conservatives hate Congress in particular because, even in the current sorry state of American politics, Congress is the place where the people can have the most influence. Every American has a local House member. Citizens can call their representatives' and senators' offices—and members of Congress keep careful count of the calls, letters, and e-mails they get. Congress has been the source of much progressive legislation. Conservatives hate the idea of expanded protections against discrimination, or effective environmental regulation, or of protection for workers' rights. So they promulgate the myth that Congress should be the least powerful branch of a feeble national government, with the courts and the executive above it, and the states above them. That idea is ridiculous in terms of the document, a flat contradiction of the history, and a patently unworkable plan for running a modern nation.

And that, from the evidence of the historical record and the text, was the "purpose" of the Constitution—to create a government with adequate power, even under new circumstances, to make the United States what George Washington, in his final address as commander of the Continental Army, called "a respectable nation."

The current war on federal power, like the other attacks on its power throughout history, is really motivated by an entirely realistic fear that those idiots, the people, will enact progressive legislation. Only by writing secret prohibitions on Congress into the Constitution can that terrible outcome be prevented.

But the more tightly we bind Congress with imaginary chains, the less we, the people, can create a "respectable nation."

CHAPTER 3

Congress Has Stretched the Commerce Power Beyond Its Proper Limits

"Our understanding of the Commerce Clause has become so broad that I often will say, if my shoes were made in Tennessee, they'll regulate my walking in Kentucky," Senator Rand Paul told the Conservative Political Action Committee Annual Convention in February 2011. Things are so bad, he added, that "recently Senator Coburn in one of the committee hearings asked Elena Kagan, he said, 'Well, do you think the government through the Commerce Clause could regulate that you eat three vegetables a day?' Her response was, 'Yes.'"[1]

The audience audibly gasped and groaned. Who knew the rot had progressed so far? Only heroes like Rand Paul stand between ordinary Americans and broccoli-wielding social engineers like Elena Kagan.

We can draw two conclusions from this. The first is that young Dr. Paul doesn't understand the Constitution. No surprise there: apple, tree, etc.

But the second thing is a bit more surprising: either Dr. Paul doesn't know truth from falsehood or he doesn't care.

Elena Kagan never said any such thing.

I know. I was at the hearing when the question was asked. Rand Paul wasn't in the room, but that's no excuse—the full transcript of the hearings is available.

Here's the actual exchange Paul misrepresented:

> Senator Coburn: If I wanted to sponsor a bill and it said,
> Americans, you have to eat three vegetables and three fruits

every day, and I got it through Congress and it's now the law of the land, you've got to do it, does that violate the Commerce Clause?

Ms. Kagan: Sounds like a dumb law.

[Laughter.]

Immediately afterwards, she added, "But I think the question of whether it's a dumb law is different from the question of whether it's constitutional, and—and—and I think that courts would be wrong to strike down laws that they think are—are senseless just because they're senseless."[2]

Kagan's answer to Coburn was, quite properly, ridicule. Neither Coburn nor anyone else really expects Congress to pass a law like this. This exchange and the cynical way Rand Paul edited it to throw raw meat to his right-wing followers exemplify the phony nature of the Right's continued hand-wringing over Congress's use of its plenary power over "to regulate commerce with foreign nations, and among the several states, and with the Indian tribes." Turn on any AM radio, visit any right-wing website, listen to any ambitious Republican politician, and you will hear apocalyptic warnings that Congress has "stretched" the Commerce Power into an engine of tyranny, far exceeding the "original intent" of the framers; indeed, they will warn, at any moment the Federal Broccoli Inspectors will be breaking down your door to enforce new federal rules of nutrition, hygiene, and personal grooming.

Like Rand Paul's speech, the right-wing attack on the Commerce Power is a blend of half-truths and outright lies. And the proper response is the one Elena Kagan gave: it's dumb, and it deserves nothing more than laughter.

Let's be clear: The Right's real objection to the Commerce Power is that in the guise of regulating commerce Congress is regulating—commerce. Commerce, they believe, shouldn't be regulated at all. The nation they imagine would allow unbridled power to private interests to make economic decisions about worker safety, environmental pollution, energy policy, food supplies, and everything else. The framers of the Constitution, socialists that they were, didn't share that vision; they gave Congress the power to regulate. That power must be blocked.

For some reason, conservative hatred for the Commerce Power centers on food. Remember Tom Coburn's question to Elena Kagan about federally mandated vegetables? Even serious questions of public safety reduce, in the extreme right imagination, to issues about force feeding. Consider Justice Clarence Thomas's response to *Alderman v. United States*, in which the Ninth Circuit upheld a federal statute that makes it a crime for violent felons to possess police-style body armor if the armor has been "sold or offered for sale, in interstate or foreign commerce." The statute's language is highly respectful of recent Supreme Court precedent, and requires the federal government to prove at trial that the armor isn't homemade in the defendant's basement.

The defendant had been arrested when he showed up for a drug-sale sting conducted by federal agents. He had the armor strapped on—almost as if he expected to be exchanging gunfire with someone. After his conviction, he appealed his conviction to the Ninth Circuit, arguing that regulation of body armor exceeded the Commerce Power. The Court of Appeals upheld the statute. The defendant petitioned the Supreme Court, which denied review.

Justice Thomas, however, filed a furious dissent from that denial, demanding that the regulation of body armor be returned to where the framers surely planned for it to be when they looked into the future and prophesied Kevlar: the states. If the federal government can protect law-enforcement personnel by denying body armor to violent felons, he said, the result will be danger to our (not making this up) *snack choices*. Thomas quoted a lower court judge warning that Congress "could outlaw 'the theft of a Hershey kiss from a corner store in Youngstown, Ohio, by a neighborhood juvenile on the basis that the candy once traveled . . . to the store from Hershey, Pennsylvania.'" Then he added that "the Government actually conceded at oral argument in the Ninth Circuit that Congress could ban possession of French fries that have been offered for sale in interstate commerce."[3]

The government is going to criminalize a stolen piece of candy? Jackbooted thugs will be peeling French fries from our cold dead hands?

Sounds like dumb law, right?

And that's the point. The Comprehensive National French Fry and Chocolate Reform Act, if any member of Congress is pixilated enough to introduce it, will die a rapid and ignominious death on some committee-room floor.

That's not an irrelevant response. The structure of the federal government and its accountability through the political process are precisely the mechanisms that the framers of the Constitution designed to prevent the federal government from overreaching its powers. Congress sometimes makes dumb laws, but surprisingly few of them would snatch away Clarence Thomas's French fries.

The constant warnings against the candy police are actually a cover for a much more troubling agenda: destroying the federal government's power to run the national economy, provide protection of the environment, and guarantee basic equality to American citizens.

To underline the stakes, consider that, as a Senate candidate, Rand Paul rather incautiously revealed that he thinks the public accommodations provisions of the Civil Rights Act of 1964—which bar owners of hotels, restaurants, theaters, and other businesses from excluding non-whites—are unconstitutional because they interfere with property rights. "Does the owner of the restaurant own his restaurant?" he asked Rachel Maddow. "Or does the government own his restaurant?"[4]

Paul's dislike of civil rights laws runs in the family. In 2004, his father, Representative Ron Paul, cast the lone House vote against a resolution praising the fortieth anniversary of the 1964 act. "The Civil Rights Act of 1964 gave the federal government unprecedented power over the hiring, employee relations, and customer service practices of every business in the country," the elder Paul complained.[5]

Bear in mind that the Civil Rights Act depended on the Commerce Power, in large part because an earlier reactionary Supreme Court disabled the Civil Rights Act of 1875. That statute had relied on the Fourteenth Amendment, with its guarantee of "the equal protection of the laws," to outlaw private discrimination. The Court voided that far-sighted law, because, it said, "private" discrimination was not action by the state government. Thus, nearly a century later, Congress had to turn to the Commerce Power as a means of dismantling Southern apartheid. Without that Commerce Power, Southern stores could still legally hang "White Only" signs in their windows.

The Commerce Power is also the basis of federal statutes outlawing employment discrimination against women, the disabled, and the elderly. The Environmental Protection Agency, the Consumer Product Safety Commission, the Food and Drug Administration, the Securities and Exchange Commission—in short, all the agencies that enable the United States to maintain a modern economy and society—stem from the Commerce Power.

Is that an overreach? The Constitution gives Congress power over "commerce with foreign nations, and among the several states, and with the Indian tribes"; is there some hidden meaning in those words that says it can't regulate "private business"? How is "commerce" carried on except by private business? How can it be "regulated" except by limits on private business?

The only way this narrow reading can be justified is by Da Vinci Code originalism, substituting other words for "commerce." That's the Clarence Thomas approach. "At the time the original Constitution was ratified, 'commerce' consisted of selling, buying, and bartering, as well as transporting for these purposes," Thomas wrote in his concurrence in *United States v. Lopez.* "The Constitution not only uses the word 'commerce' in a narrower sense than our case law might suggest, it also does not support the proposition that Congress has authority over all activities that 'substantially affect' interstate commerce."[6]

Under this definition, Congress would not be able to regulate either growing crops for sale on world markets or the manufacture of goods for sale in the national economy. It wouldn't be able to reach air and water pollution, or toxic waste, generated by factories or farms. It wouldn't be able to regulate sale or possession of illegal drugs or possession of child pornography. It's hard to see how it could reach "private" discrimination against anyone.

Thomas claims that "the original understanding" of the clause was narrow. As Yale scholar Jack Balkin points out, Thomas's quotations from eighteenth-century dictionaries were carefully edited. Thomas quoted Samuel Johnson's *Dictionary of the English Language*, but carefully left out the quotation Samuel Johnson used to illustrate the term, which spoke of churches as places for "*commerce* to be had between God and us."[7] Did the Founders sell, buy, or barter with God? Balkin's colleague Akhil Amar has written that "'commerce' also had in 1787, and retains even now, a broader meaning referring to all forms of intercourse in the affairs of life, whether or not narrowly economic or mediated by explicit markets."[8]

The most influential early interpretation of the word "commerce" came from John Marshall, fourth chief justice of the United States. Marshall is frequently the target of "Pay No Attention to That Man Behind the Curtain" originalists. They portray him as a sinister interloper waging war against "original intent." Conservative historian Kevin R. C. Gutzman sums up their case neatly: "the Philadelphia Convention, the ratification process, the Tenth Amendment, and the political defeat of the Federalist Party . . . were all undone by the Marshall Court."[9]

What they often don't point out is that Marshall also has strong credentials as a Founder—stronger, for example, than those of Tea Party darling Thomas Jefferson, who was absent from the United States during the framing and ratification of the Constitution. Marshall, by contrast, was a delegate to the Virginia ratifying convention in 1788 and, along with James Madison and Edmund Randolph, a floor leader in the fight for ratification. George Washington personally begged him to run for Congress, and when he was elected, President John Adams appointed him secretary of state and then chief justice. In that role, Marshall insisted that the framers and ratifiers of the Constitution had created a strong federal government, armed with power to repel attempts by any state to block its regulation of commerce.

In *Gibbons v. Ogden*, the first major case to test the Commerce Power, Marshall used the same definition of "commerce" as Samuel Johnson's number two (the one which Clarence Thomas omitted): "Commerce, undoubtedly, is traffic, but it is something more: it is intercourse. It describes the commercial intercourse between nations, and parts of nations, in all its branches, and is regulated by prescribing rules for carrying on that intercourse." How much "intercourse" could the Commerce Power reach? "The subject to which the power is next applied is to commerce 'among the several States,'" Marshall explained. "The word 'among' means intermingled with. A thing which is among others is intermingled with them. Commerce among the States cannot stop at the external boundary line of each State, but may be introduced into the interior."

Marshall was careful to say that there was *probably* some kind of "commerce" that Congress couldn't reach: "It is not intended to say that these words comprehend that commerce which is completely internal, which is carried on between man and man in a State, or between different parts of the same State, and which does not extend to or affect other States. Such a power would be inconvenient, and is certainly unnecessary. . . . Comprehensive as the word 'among' is, it may very properly be restricted to that commerce which concerns more States than one."[10]

Two things are striking about this early interpretation by a Founder. First, "commerce which concerns more States than one" tracks almost exactly the definition Justice Thomas angrily rejects—"all activities that 'substantially affect' interstate commerce." Second, Marshall's definition of that subset of "commerce" that Congress may *not* regulate is very narrow: "between man and man," suggesting that larger-scale business would not be exempt; completely within a state, meaning that there was no actual crossing of state lines; and not "extend[ing] to or affect[ing] other states," meaning that even if it is small scale or internal, it must not affect the larger market. That would exclude a kid's lemonade stand (or a chocolate shoplifter), but it would still provide plenty of power by which Congress could regulate an entire national market.

I quote Marshall at length not because he's infallible or because the quotes somehow prove that every Founder had the same "intent" or "understanding" when the Commerce Clause was framed and ratified. Marshall's words, and the sum of his jurisprudence as chief justice, do, however, reveal the dishonesty of right-wing claims that we have somehow "strayed" from the "original meaning" of the Commerce Power and that their project is to "restore" its original purity.

In fact, the definition they favor comes from a time much later than the Founding—a time that history has not judged kindly: the Gilded Age of robber barons and "survival of the fittest." They praise Supreme Court decisions reached by the Gilded Age Court of the late nineteenth century and the "Lochner era" Court of the early twentieth. In those cases, justices freely redefined "commerce" to exclude agriculture, manufacturing, hiring, firing, wages, child labor—any aspect of business that they, following a nineteenth-century philosophy of *laissez faire*, believed should be free of regulation. That hostility, in fact, wasn't even really based on federalism or on the limits of the Commerce Power; at the same time these Courts were striking down federal regulations of labor and wages, they were invalidating those same measures when passed by *states*—on the grounds that they interfered with the "natural rights" of "freedom of contract" and unregulated use of private property.

These are Clarence Thomas's good old days: sweatshops, firetrap factories, lawless strikebreaking thugs, and child labor. The Right can't get us back there by following any real claim of "original intent." It will take serious judicial rewriting of the Constitution and the case law to do it.

Does that really mean there are "no limits" on Congress's power? Will the next sound you hear be the Fries Police bellowing over a bullhorn, "Back away from the malt-vinegar bottle"?

No.

First, the current Court, in a series of decisions in the late 1990s, has put one limit on congressional statutes based on the Commerce Power.

They must, it held, be regulations of "commercial activity" in some way. In a case called *United States v. Lopez*, the Court struck down a "Gun-Free School Zones Act" that made no reference to commerce, but simply outlawed all guns near schools.[11] In *United States v. Morrison*, the Court invalidated a portion of the Violence Against Women Act that created a federal "cause of action," or basis for civil lawsuit, by victims of gender-based violence against their abusers.[12] In neither case, the Court said, was Congress regulating a larger market, and the statute itself (unlike the body-armor statute in *Alderman*, which we discussed above) did not make relation to interstate commerce a necessary element of the offense.

That provides a pretty clear guide to future Congresses who want to draft valid regulations of commerce. The hypothetical "chocolate theft" statute, as a pure regulation of noneconomic local crime, would not pass muster: under *Lopez*, it would be an interference with purely local law enforcement. Same for the dreaded French-fry possession ban.

There's a second, more important, limit. It's the one Justice Kagan pointed out. Either of the hypothetical laws would be dumb laws. It's hard to imagine any Congress passing either.

But they might, surely, and surely that possibility should frighten us? Why? We can invent hideous hypothetical abuses of any congressional power. Congress could use its power to "raise and support armies" to draft all able-bodied adults into the Marine Band. It could use its power to build "post roads" to pave over Yosemite. It could use the Sixteenth Amendment income-tax power to impose a 110 percent tax rate on every person in America. It could use its power to "fix the standard of weights and measures" to make one inch equal to the length of Lady Gaga's nose. Nothing in the text of the Constitution forbids any of these laws.

But they won't happen. Those would be dumb laws, and the political structure created by the Constitution—two houses of Congress responsible to the voters, and a president armed with the power of the veto—would stop them before they got started. That political structure is the primary defense the framers intended as protection against federal overreach.

The real concern of the Pauls and Thomases is not with dumb laws; it is with ones that aren't so dumb. As I am writing this, the major Commerce Clause dispute is not over French fry regulation but over the Affordable Care Act and its "individual mandate" that every taxpayer buy health insurance coverage or pay a tax penalty.

Some people think the "mandate" is a good idea. (As a matter of historical fact, the "mandate" was originally a *conservative* idea, designed to prevent the creation of a massive new government program and to emphasize the requirement of "personal responsibility." Mitt Romney was for the "mandate" before he was against it.) Others think it didn't go far enough—that a federal "single payer" system would do a better job of providing coverage for the uninsured. And some think we should have no federal health insurance program at all.

But what I think, or you think, or Clarence Thomas thinks is the *best* way to handle health care isn't the issue. The *constitutional* issue is this: Can anyone with a straight face argue that regulating health care, and the way individuals pay for it, is somehow *not* regulating "commerce which concerns more States than one"? The Far Right used to warn that the health care bill was a "takeover" of "one-sixth of the national economy"; now it has turned on a dime to argue that it's not "commerce" at all.

By the time you have read this, the Supreme Court may have decided that the "mandate" doesn't pass muster. If it does, that decision will be a triumph for the Rand Paul–Clarence Thomas view and, unless progressives mobilize, could mark the first step backward toward their Waldorf & Statler dystopia of unregulated mines and mills.

And that would be "dumb law" indeed.

CHAPTER 4

The Constitution Doesn't Separate Church and State

Christine O'Donnell of Delaware was one of the most talked-about Tea Party Senate candidates in the fall of 2010. O'Donnell in her youth had been an anti-masturbation activist and had, she said, "dabbled into witch-craft."[1] By 2010, though, she was firmly established on the Christian right, with a Tea Party platform as far to the right as any of the Republican candidates in that year's carnival of extremism. O'Donnell's campaign self-destructed, however, in a memorable debate with her Democratic opponent, Chris Coons.

O'Donnell suggested that local school districts should be free to teach "creationism"—the doctrine that God made the earth and created humans and all the animals. Coons told her that such state-imposed religious doctrine in schools would violate the First Amendment's prohibition against "an establishment of religion." The following dialogue ensued:

> O'Donnell: Let me just clarify: You're telling me that the separation of church and state is found in the First Amendment?
>
> Coons: Government shall make no establishment of religion.
>
> O'Donnell: That's in the First Amendment?[2]

An audience of law students audibly gasped. O'Donnell didn't even know the words of the Constitution when she heard them. She paid for her ignorance with a thumping repudiation at the polls. But her mistake was not a random one, and her cohorts on the right rushed to her defense. As Rush Limbaugh explained, "She was incredulous that somebody was saying that the Constitution said there must be separation between church and state. Those words are not in the Constitution."[3]

The far-right attack on separation of church and state is of a very specific kind. The idea is that the Founders were devout Christians, and that their "original intent" has been deliberately covered up by sinister secular forces in the twentieth century. Like a fundamentalist attacking a German "higher critic," Newt Gingrich warned an audience in 2011 that "the American elites are guided by their desire to emulate the European elites and, as a result, anti-religious values and principles are coming to dominate the academic, news media, and judicial class in America."[4]

These "elites" are also at work in the public schools. In 2006, Michele Bachmann warned a Christian group that schools "are teaching children that there is separation of church and state, and I am here to tell you that is a myth."[5]

The attack on separation involves twisting words and reading history backward, and it involves making some inconvenient parts of the Constitution disappear. Most ardently espoused by loud foes of "big government," the attack aims to place that big government in charge of Americans' spiritual lives.

The idea is that the framers desired a "Christian nation," in which government oversaw the spiritual development of the people by reminding them of their religious duties and subsidizing the churches where they worship. "Establishment of religion," in this strange reading, simply means that no single Christian *denomination* could be officially favored. But official prayers, exhortations to faith, religious monuments, federal funding for religious schools and programs, and participation by church bodies in government were all part of the "original intent," the argument goes. Anything goes as long as government does not legally punish anyone for not taking part in state-sponsored religious exercises.

Because the *words* "separation of church and state" do not appear in the Constitution, the argument runs, the document provides for *merger* of the two.

There's a second part of the argument. Because the First Amendment, when adopted in the eighteenth century, only restricted the federal government, the enemies of separation suggest that it still does not restrict state governments—which are free to involve themselves with religion in any way they want, from school prayer all the way to designating an official state religion. Remarkably enough, those advancing this view simply ignore the Fourteenth Amendment (see Myth 8), which has made the Establishment and Free Exercise Clauses applicable to every government in America.

These twin arguments are among the most flamboyantly dishonest deployed by today's Right, which has forged a complete alternative history of America to support it. It is bosh: ahistorical, antitextual, and illogical.

The current attack on separation began in the 1980s as an attack on a letter by Thomas Jefferson to the Danbury Baptist Association, dated January 1, 1802. As president, Jefferson assured the Baptists that "I contemplate with sovereign reverence that act of the whole American people which declared that their legislature should 'make no law respecting an establishment of religion, or prohibiting the free exercise thereof,' thus building a wall of separation between Church & State."[6]

In 1985, then Justice William Rehnquist wrote that "unfortunately the Establishment Clause has been expressly freighted with Jefferson's misleading metaphor for nearly 40 years."[7] The idea is that opponents of state-sponsored religion have seized on a random phrase of Jefferson's and tortured it far beyond what it actually said, and further, that the idea of "separation" was only in Jefferson's mind, and had no roots in the thought of the Founders.

But this argument ignores a historical fact. It's not Jefferson's metaphor. Even in 1802, both the term "wall of separation" and the idea it represented were already deeply rooted in American religious history. In 1644, the American theologian Roger Williams, founder of the first Baptist congregation in the British New World, coined the phrase to signify the protection that the church needed in order to prevent misuse and corruption by political leaders: "The church of the Jews under the Old Testament in the type and the church of the Christians under the New Testament in the antitype were both separate from the world; and when they have opened a gap in the hedge or wall of separation between the garden of the church and the wilderness of the world, God hath ever broke down the wall itself, removed the candlestick, and made his garden a wilderness."[8]

Williams was resolutely devout—at the age of seventy, he rowed himself thirty miles in order to debate theology with a group of Quakers. But he was equally uncompromising in his determination that Rhode Island "might be a shelter for persons distressed for conscience."[9] The persecution had come at the hands of the Puritans in Massachusetts, who saw no reason why the state shouldn't bring souls to God by giving heretical bodies a good whipping, a sojourn in the stocks or prison, or even hanging. Rhode Island's first charter, in 1647, showed Williams's influence when it declared that "all men may walk as their consciences persuade them, every one in the name of his God."[10] (This language foreshadowed the thought of James Madison, the leading theorist of church and state under the Constitution, whose original Bill of Rights contained a provision protecting "the equal rights of conscience" against all governments, state or federal.)

Over the next century and a half, the Baptist tradition became well acquainted with persecution by other Christians wielding the sword of the state. (In fact, it was the imprisonment of a group of Baptist preachers by the authorities in Virginia's Orange County that set the young James Madison on his lifelong quest for religious liberty and divorce between church and state.) In referring to "the wall of separation," Jefferson was not only paying a graceful tribute to the history of the Danbury Baptist congregation but also evoking an idea well rooted in American thought.

Following Rehnquist's lead, the Far Right has attempted to erase the long history of an American idea that has been adopted in many other parts of the world. Amateur historian David Barton devotes his book *Original Intent: The Courts, The Constitution, and Religion* to the proposition that separation of church and state is "a relatively recent concept rather than . . . a long-standing constitutional principle."[11]

Barton has transformed himself into a cottage industry, self-publishing books claiming that the "original intent" of the "Founding Fathers" was that America would be a Christian nation in which political power and office would be held by Protestant Christians, and the state would attempt to point straying sheep the way to heaven.

In a saner age, Barton would be peddling his ideas on street corners. But in the heated atmosphere of 2012, he has become an adviser to Michele Bachmann and to Newt Gingrich, who promised to consult Barton if he became president. Mike Huckabee praises him as "maybe the greatest living historian on the spiritual nature of America's early days."[12]

In point of fact, Barton isn't a historian at all. His educational credentials consist of a BA in religious education from Oral Roberts University. His thick volumes are published by his own organization, WallBuilders, which is "dedicated to presenting America's forgotten history and heroes, with an emphasis on the moral, religious, and constitutional foundation on which America was built—a foundation which, in recent years, has been seriously attacked and undermined."[13] What this "foundation" consists of, from the evidence of Barton's books and websites, is government endorsement of Christianity and sponsorship of official prayers.

Barton's historical "method" consists mostly of assembling page after page of quotations from Americans, famous or obscure, from the Founding period. These quotes invariably praise Christianity as the greatest religion in the world and suggest that America cannot prosper unless its people hew to Christian values. From this mass of quotations, Barton then engages in a variety of "originalisms"—Da Vinci Code originalism, in which he explains that the text of the Constitution doesn't mean what it says, and Man Behind the Curtain originalism, in which he explains that any quotations from Founders contradicting his view actually don't count.

So far, I've just described the work of a man who is sloppy and untrained. And heaven knows Barton's knowledge of history and the world contains astonishing gaps. Like most humorless fanatics, he sees the world as full of sinister enemies at work to subvert the truth. For example, he denounces the famous Broadway musical *1776*, which was later made into a film. Anyone who's ever seen this show recognizes it as a fond, satirical retelling of the story of the Declaration of Independence, a silly fantasy in which Thomas Jefferson, John Adams, and Benjamin Franklin dance around the stage and sing songs with titles like "Cool, Cool Considerate Men" or "Piddle, Twiddle, and Resolve."

Barton, like all true fanatics, lacks any sense that there may be humor or affectionate satire in the world. He is outraged at a scene that portrays Jefferson as so eager to go to bed with his wife that he is unable to finish drafting the Declaration of Independence. He has convinced himself that this is a part of a conspiracy to convince Americans that the framers were licentious and corrupt. Of this and other humorous dialogue in the play, he sniffs, "there is absolutely no evidence to support any of these exchanges."[14]

If Barton were merely an ignorant, half-educated zealot, the attention paid to his "research" by serious political figures would be scandal enough. But in point of fact, he is more than a crackpot; he is a charlatan, who systematically misrepresents his source material to throw dust in the reader's eyes.

Consider this discussion of the framing of the First Amendment in Barton's 2007 pamphlet, *Separation of Church and State: What the Founders Meant:*

> The *Congressional Record* (required by the Constitution in Art. I Sec. 5 ¶3) contains all the official words and acts that occur in congressional chambers. Those records therefore include the discussion of the ninety Founders in the first federal Congress who, from June 8 to September 25, 1789, framed the First Amendment. In those lengthy discussions that spanned months, the Founders repeatedly explained that they were seeking to prevent what they had experienced under Great Britain: the legal establishment by the national government of a single religious denomination in exclusion of all others (whether Catholic, Anglican, or any other). Very simply, their oft-repeated intent was that Congress could not officially establish any one denomination in America; or, in the wording proposed by James Madison, "nor shall any *national* religion be established."[15]

What conclusion would you draw from this about the evidence Barton claims to be relying on? It certainly sounds like the (1) official (2) *Congressional Record* contains (3) months of debate by (4) nearly one hundred speakers over the meaning of the First Amendment. That implication is deepened by a deceptive footnote attached to this paragraph, which cites a record of debates spanning 512 pages.

But each of the numbered statements above is false, and each seems to have been carefully written to mislead the reader. First, "Art. I Sec. 5 ¶3" of the Constitution does *not* require the creation of the *Congressional Record* or any other record of congressional debates. All it requires is that "each House shall keep a *journal* of its proceedings"—meaning a relatively brief notation of each bill, measure, and motion passed, with a recording of the vote and, when a member requested it, a list of who had voted "yea" and "nay." (If you want to see the actual Journal of the First Congress, it's readily available on the Library of Congress website.[16]) There was (and is) no constitutional requirement that the government transcribe and publish the debates in Congress. In fact, the First Congress, which passed the First Amendment, did not do so.

The *Congressional Record,* which Barton claims to be quoting, was not established until 1873. Barton's footnote, in fact, is not to the *Con-*

gressional Record (how could it be?) but to a volume called *Debates and Proceedings in the Congress of the United States*, which was a collection of newspaper accounts of what transpired. The *Debates and Proceedings* was not assembled and published until 1834, long after most of the speakers were dead. Further, the *Debates and Proceedings* wasn't an official government publication; its volumes were assembled by a private publisher.

It's bad enough to misrepresent the source, but Barton also misrepresents what the source says. These weren't "lengthy discussions that spanned months." The Framing of the Bill of Rights did take place between June and September 1789, but it took place by fits and starts, amid debates and votes on other urgent legislation. The 500-plus pages he "cites" in his footnote are actually mostly filled with discussions about other things. In fact, the records of debate on the First Amendment religion clauses occupy only about 20 pages in *The Complete Bill of Rights: The Drafts, Debates, Sources & Origins* by Neil H. Cogan, an actual scholar who carefully documents the debates.[17] Remember those "ninety Founders" who supposedly debated for those five months? The *Records* actually quote only *eight* members of Congress as speaking on the Religion Clauses at all.

Equally remarkably, Barton omits one specific proposal that Madison did make in the First Congress. That proposal would have applied separationist concepts—which Barton claims only concern the federal government—against the states as well. That article of the proposed bill of rights reads, "No state shall violate the equal rights of conscience, or the freedom of the press, or the trial by jury in criminal cases."[18] Though this proposal failed to achieve ratification, it's an important indication of Madison's own mind, and it suggests that he would not have "very simply" favored continuation of state-established religion.

I am sorry to say this, but I am unable to believe that any literate human being is ham-fisted enough to misrepresent a written record so badly *by mistake*. Barton is an American type as old as Mark Twain's Duke and Dauphin in *Huckleberry Finn*: a snake-oil salesman compiling a tissue of falsehoods to mislead those too busy to read actual history or too credulous to question his dubious claims and nonexistent credentials. That Republican politicians have relied on this charlatan, and continue to do so, says all that need be said about their intellectual integrity or their understanding of American history.

Barton may fool the rubes, but he needn't fool the rest of us. And no one should be fooled by the rest of the Right's catalog of misrepresentations about the First Amendment and religion. The truth is far more complex. The Founding generation's opinions on religion cover a wide span, running all the way from orthodoxy to almost total infidelity. The First Amendment protected all those opinions, and in no way aimed at setting up a "Christian nation" where government would guide souls to Christ.

Many patriots like Thomas Jefferson and James Madison were profoundly skeptical about the claims of what they called "revealed religion." As children of the eighteenth-century Enlightenment, many of them stressed reason and scientific observation as a means of discovering the nature of "Providence," the power that had created the world. This is the belief that is called deism. The world, the deist argument ran, was so complex that only a designer could have made it. By studying the design we would learn about the designer. The "revelations" in books like the Bible were neither true nor necessary to religious understanding. The truth about Providence and humanity was to be found by reason studying evidence, not faith reading scripture.

Jefferson, for example, was clearly not a Christian of a kind that today's evangelical churches would recognize. He took a pair of scissors to the Christian New Testament and cut out every passage that suggested a divine origin and mission for Jesus. Jefferson's "Bible," which he titled *The Life and Morals of Jesus of Nazareth Extracted Textually from the Gospels*, ends with the words "Now in the place where he was crucified there was a garden; and in the garden a new sepulchre, wherein was never man yet laid. There laid they Jesus, And rolled a great stone to the door of the sepulchre, and departed."[19] That's it. No Easter, no Resurrection, no founding of the Church, no Ascension. In 1822, Jefferson wrote to a friend that Christianity would probably die out. "I rejoice that in this blessed country of free inquiry and belief, which has surrendered its conscience to neither kings or priests, the genuine doctrine of only one God is reviving, and I trust that there is not a young man now living in the United States who will not die a Unitarian."[20]

In their long correspondence, Jefferson and John Adams swapped frequent witticisms about the presumption of the clergy. ("Every Species of these Christians would persecute Deists," Adams wrote on June 25, 1813, "as soon as either Sect would persecute another, if it had unchecked and unbalanced power. Nay, the Deists would persecute Christians, and Atheists would persecute Deists, with as unrelenting Cruelty, as any Christians would persecute them or one another. Know thyself, Human Nature!"[21])

Adams himself was probably more favorably inclined toward organized Christianity than Jefferson, but as president, Adams signed (and the U.S. Senate approved) the 1797 Treaty with Tripoli, which reassured that Muslim nation that "the Government of the United States of America is not, in any sense, founded on the Christian religion."[22]

James Madison, the father of both the Constitution and the First Amendment, consistently warned against any attempt to blend endorsement of Christianity into the law of the new nation. "Who does not see that the same authority which can establish Christianity, in exclusion of all other Religions," he wrote in his "Memorial and Remonstrance against Religious Assessments" in 1785, "may establish with the same ease any particular sect of Christians, in exclusion of all other Sects?"[23]

Unlike the Articles of Confederation, the Constitution's text conspicuously omits any reference to God. The words "separation of church and state" are not in the text, but the idea of separation is. In fact, separation was there before the First Amendment was added: Article VI provides that all state and federal officials "shall be bound by oath or affirmation, to support this Constitution; but *no religious test shall ever be required* as a qualification to any office or public trust under the United States." This was an important change—in England, officeholders had to be members of a state-approved church and take an oath, invoking God's name, to support it.

Barton deals with this inconvenient clause by invoking Da Vinci Code originalism: to the untutored eye, it seems to say that officeholders could not be asked about their religious beliefs, if any, but actually "means" that "the Constitution required an oath of office, but prohibited a religious test; an oath, however, presupposed a belief in God; therefore, only under the most extreme and absurd application of Article VI could a belief in God have been considered a religious test."[24] Thus, only those who believe in God can hold office. Ingenious, I suppose, were it not for the fact that the Constitution also explicitly allowed anyone who objected to the oath to use "affirmation" instead.[25] Then, and now, "affirmation" was a term at law meaning "A formal and solemn declaration, having the same weight and invested with the same responsibilities as an oath, by persons who conscientiously decline taking an oath"—such as, for example, because they don't believe in God.[26] Having Da Vinci Coded a *bar* on religious tests into a *religious test* in itself, Barton goes further. In his world, a belief in God wasn't enough. The framers didn't want *Catholics* holding office either, because they maintained a "sworn oath of allegiance to a 'foreign power' (the pope)."[27]

In fact, the religious test clause was a radical separationist provision; the First Congress soon added the First Amendment's Establishment Clause (which Christine O'Donnell had apparently not read). It provides that "Congress shall make no law respecting an establishment of religion." That last choice of words suggests that not only no church but also no "religion" could be made the official faith of the United States. (To Barton and others on the Christian right, this simply means that the federal government was to favor all forms of *Protestantism* equally.) Finally, the Free Exercise Clause provides that Congress shall not make laws "prohibiting the free exercise" of religion. So government could not prohibit the practice of minority religions either.

Despite Madison's best efforts to protect "the equal rights of conscience" against state governments, the First Amendment prohibitions at first only ran against the federal government. But in 1868, the Fourteenth Amendment extended the protections of the Bill of Rights to the state governments. Barton and his ilk refuse to recognize the Fourteenth Amendment as anything but a charter of "racial civil rights."[28] (As we will see later, this Fourteenth Amendment denial is an essential claim of those who want to take the United States back to something like the Articles of Confederation.)

But here is the law today: the government can't require its officials to support a church or hold any religious belief at all; may not support a church, or religion generally, itself; and may not interfere with the worship or belief of any church. Is there a serious argument that church and state are *not* separate?

As children of the Enlightenment, the framing generation was well aware that the use by political leaders of religion for their own ends was a danger both to the faithful and to the peace of society. The Constitution embodies that idea. The current right-wing drive to harness the power of government to bring souls to Christ is dangerous and un-American. Anyone who has read a newspaper in the last decade understands that when governments and political groups begin to act in the name of God, persecution, martyrdom, and civil war are never far away. It should take more than phony footnotes and deceptive quotes about "original intent" to persuade us as a people to turn our souls over to the state, or the Republican Party, for protection.

Some evangelical and conservative Christians, who owe their own religious freedom as much to Roger Williams as to James Madison, are now ready to abandon that history. This change calls to mind the story of Esau, older son of Isaac in the Bible. One day, from momentary hunger, Esau foolishly exchanged the rich inheritance that awaited him—land and cattle—for the immediate satisfaction of a bowl of lentils. When God later called him to account for selling his birthright, the Book of Genesis tells us, Esau "lifted up his voice, and wept."[29]

Many American Christians being fed the "Christian America" idea may do the same if the fearsome theocracy of Bachmann, Barton, and Gingrich ever comes to pass. As no less conservative a figure than Sandra Day O'Connor wrote in 2005, "Those who would renegotiate the boundaries between church and state must therefore answer a difficult question: why would we trade a system that has served us so well for one that has served others so poorly?"[30]

CHAPTER 5

Equality and Self-Government Are "Wholly Foreign to the First Amendment"

Our political system is in trouble. To understand why, consider the following question posed from the bench by Chief Justice John Roberts during oral argument in a campaign-finance case, *Arizona Free Enterprise Club's Freedom Club PAC v. Bennett*.[1]

In 1998, the voters of Arizona created a voluntary public-financing system, in which a candidate who agreed not to solicit or spend private funds would receive state funding to run a competitive campaign. Public financing is a great idea, but privately financed candidates can often raise much more than the amount allotted to their challengers by the state, and thus drown out publicly financed candidates. To address this concern, the act provided that if a privately financed candidate spent more than a publicly financed candidate's allotted funding, the publicly financed candidate would receive additional funds to allow a competitive election.

Right-wing political groups challenged the provision allowing additional funding. The increased funding for publicly financed candidates, they argued, infringed the free-speech rights of privately financed candidates. Those candidates, poor babies, would be discouraged from speaking because their opponents might be able to answer them.

When the case came before the Court, Roberts asked the state of Arizona's lawyer, "I checked the Citizens' Clean Elections Commission website this morning, and it says that this act was passed to, quote, 'level the playing field' when it comes to running for office. Why isn't that clear evidence that it's unconstitutional?"[2]

Every law student learns that appellate judges are not supposed to go Googling around in search of new evidence to spring on counsel during oral argument. Appellate judges are supposed to decide cases only on the record before the Court. Early in 2012, when a government lawyer defending environmental regulations seemed to be straying from the printed record of evidence, Roberts dressed him down in front of the audience in the Supreme Court chamber: "If they weren't in the record, I don't want to hear about them. You appreciate that rule, that we don't consider things that aren't in the record."[3] That same rule apparently doesn't apply when the chief justice wants to take down a progressive campaign-finance rule. Roberts's Internet search seems almost like "judicial hacktivism."

But beyond that obvious impropriety, the chief justice's nose for heresy would do credit to the Spanish Inquisition. Any hint of the idea of civic equality, any thought of a "level playing field," was to him proof that the entire election scheme (which the Court duly invalidated three months later) was invalid. The Republican right wing, and the conservative majority on the Supreme Court, have decided over the past forty years that freedom of speech is a weapon of social control, not a tool of self-government. That distortion has done severe damage to our democracy and threatens to destroy it.

In 2009, the United States Supreme Court held that corporations must be given the right to fund unlimited amounts of advertising advocating the election or defeat of political candidates. In *Citizens United v. Federal Election Commission*,[4] the Court gutted the McCain-Feingold Act, the first significant (even if timid) attempt at campaign finance reform since the laws passed in the wake of the Watergate scandals.

The ban on "independent expenditures" was designed to avoid giving ordinary citizens the impression that wealthy people and organizations can buy influence with the candidates they support. The Court, however, laughed off this aim. "Independent expenditures, including those made by corporations, do not give rise to corruption or the appearance of corruption," Justice Anthony Kennedy wrote for the majority. "The appearance of influence or access, furthermore, will not cause the electorate to lose faith in our democracy."[5] The Court did not deign to explain where it was getting its information about public attitudes. Given the current cynicism among the public about the role of money in politics, this statement seems almost breathtakingly wrong-headed.

What *Citizens United* means is that corporations and wealthy donors, with their enormous financial resources, can flood the airwaves with ads from deceptively titled "issue groups" with names like "Americans for Prosperity" and "American Future Funds." This is precisely what happened in the 2010 campaign, when these anonymous funds swamped Democratic and progressive candidates with semi-anonymous attack ads in the days before the election. Perhaps coincidentally, those elections produced a radical shift to the right in the membership of both the House and the Senate. The same thing has now happened even to Republicans during the early primaries of 2012, when anonymously funded "super PACs" allied with Mitt Romney and Newt Gingrich poured millions into small-state contests to attack their candidates' rivals. In February 2012, the Obama campaign bowed to the inevitable and began urging wealthy donors to support its own super PAC, Priorities USA Action. The political arms race and the influence of the wealthy over politics are bound to assume a new and monstrous level as the 2012 campaign cycle moves forward.

And the activists of the Right are ready with cases designed to push corporate domination further. In a case called *United States v. Danielczyk*, District Judge James C. Cacheris held that even the current federal ban of direct *contributions* from corporate treasuries to political candidates violates the First Amendment: "Taken seriously, *Citizens United* requires that corporations and individuals be afforded equal rights to political speech, unqualified. . . . Thus, following *Citizens United*, individuals and corporations must have equal rights to engage in *both* independent expenditures *and* direct contributions. They must have the same rights to *both* the 'apple' *and* the 'orange.'"[6]

Judge Cacheris's opinion directly contradicted what the Supreme Court had said in *Citizens United*, but there's little doubt the Court will take the contribution argument seriously when the issue comes before it. Meanwhile, right-wing lawyers are also vowing to void *any* requirement that contributors—either to super PACs or directly to the candidates themselves—disclose their identities. Somehow this would also violate their "freedom of speech."

In other words, like levees on the Mississippi, the extremely modest restrictions on corporate domination of American politics are being deliberately breached; the result, as in New Orleans in 2005, is a man-made disaster, a flood of corporate money that is distorting, and indeed threatens to destroy, American democracy.

To hear the Right discuss it, though, anyone who questions *Citizens United* is spitting on James Madison's grave. "Any proponent of free speech should applaud this decision. *Citizens United* is and will be a First Amendment triumph of enduring significance," Senator Mitch McConnell (R-KY) crowed on the Senate floor after the decision.[7] Representative Mike Pence (R-IN) also explained that "the Court has taken important steps toward restoring to the American people their First Amendment rights. This decision is a victory on behalf of those who cherish the fundamental freedoms protected by the First Amendment."[8] Senator John Cornyn (R-TX) told the *New York Times* that "I can't think of a more fundamental First Amendment issue." (He also noted that, by a bizarre coincidence, the decision would "open up resources that have not previously been available" to the Republican candidates.[9]) Even Newt Gingrich, who regards federal courts as the enemy and vowed that as president he would refuse to follow their decisions, has gone out of his way to praise the Supreme Court for "its principled defense of our First Amendment rights to freedom of speech, for example in the recent case of *Citizens United.*"[10]

Progressives and moderates have reacted differently. In his dissent in *Citizens United*, Justice John Paul Stevens—a moderate-conservative Republican—spoke for many citizens when he said, "While American democracy is imperfect, few outside the majority of this Court would have thought its flaws included a dearth of corporate money in politics."[11] In his 2010 State of the Union address, President Obama scolded the justices seated in front of him, saying, "With all due deference to separation of powers, last week the Supreme Court reversed a century of law that I believe will open the floodgates for special interests—including foreign corporations—to spend without limit in our elections."[12]

Much of the outraged reaction to *Citizens United* has centered on its premise that the First Amendment applies to political speech by corporations in precisely the same way that it does to speech by individuals. The idea has grown up that the case actually created the idea of "corporate personhood." That's because the First Amendment's guarantee of free speech applies to the states by way of the Fourteenth Amendment, which forbids the states to "deny to any *person* . . . the due process of law." Jeffrey D. Clements, general counsel and cofounder of Free Speech for People, recently published an anti–*Citizens United* book with the title *Corporations Are Not People: Why They Have More Rights Than You Do and What You Can Do About It*.[13] Demonstrators outside the Supreme Court on the second anniversary of the *Citizens United* decision put on a skit with actors wearing large boxes with corporate labels. While a chorus sang *Sesame Street*'s song about "a person in your neighborhood," the "corporate" boxes tried to blend in with a crowd of ordinary workers and consumers. "I'll Believe Corporations Are People When Texas Executes One" is the legend on one popular anti–*Citizens United* lapel button.

But the attack on "corporate personhood" misunderstands both the case and the problem with current First Amendment law. The problem is not that corporations are "persons" under the law. Corporations have always been "persons"—that is and always has been, in fact, the definition of a corporation, a "fictive person" that is able to own property and enter into legal agreements. And the problem is not the mere idea that corporate "persons" have free-speech rights. Of course they do; otherwise the government could prohibit the New York Times Co. or MSNBC from engaging in news coverage, or forbid them from endorsing candidates or criticizing government policy. The idea that corporations have some of the free-speech rights that people have is essential to the Court's important free-speech decisions, such as *New York Times v. Sullivan* and *New York Times v. United States*, which have removed the threat of government censorship from American media.

In fact, for years the idea that corporations had no free-speech rights was a conservative idea, inspired at least in part by hostility to the media. In a 1977 case called *First National Bank of Boston v. Bellotti*, the Court majority held that Massachusetts could not bar ads by a corporation opposing a public referendum affecting its taxes. Justice (later Chief Justice) William Rehnquist dissented. In an opinion that has a contemporary ring, he wrote:

> A State grants to a business corporation the blessings of potentially perpetual life and limited liability to enhance its efficiency as an economic entity. It might reasonably be concluded that those properties, so beneficial in the economic sphere, pose special dangers in the political sphere. . . . Indeed, the States might reasonably fear that the corporation would use its economic power to obtain further benefits beyond those already bestowed.[14]

That danger—that a corporation will "use its economic power to obtain further benefits"—has now come to pass. The problem is not corporate "personhood"; it is the kind of simple-minded interpretation of the Constitution I have discussed in the introduction to this book. The Court in *Citizens United* claimed to be choosing between a system in which corporations would have *no* free-speech rights and one in which corporate "persons" must have *precisely* the same free-speech rights as natural persons do.

There is a middle position. Justice Stevens himself explained it to Stephen Colbert in January. "For some purposes, corporations are persons," he said. "As with natural persons as well as corporate persons, some have different rights than others do. The same rights don't apply to everyone in every possible situation."[15]

Stevens is right—as even the majority on the Supreme Court recognizes. In 2011, the AT&T Corporation tried to bar release of some corporate documents under the Freedom of Information Act. The documents had been turned over to the Federal Communications Commission as part of an investigation; once that was concluded, FOIA required disclosure to the public. But the corporations invoked an exception in the statute for materials that would be "an unwarranted invasion of personal privacy."

Chief Justice John Roberts, writing for a unanimous Court, treated the claim with outright ridicule: "We reject the argument that because 'person' is defined for purposes of FOIA to include a corporation, the phrase 'personal privacy' in Exemption 7(C) reaches corporations as well. The protection in FOIA against disclosure of law enforcement information on the ground that it would constitute an unwarranted invasion of personal privacy does not extend to corporations. We trust that AT&T will not take it personally."[16]

Roberts has it exactly right. Our laws treat many kinds of "persons" differently for various purposes—citizens differently from noncitizens, minors differently from adults, members of professions differently from nonmembers. Each group's rights—even important rights like free speech—are treated differently for some purposes. High school students do not have the right to demonstrate against school policy during school hours; college students do. Minors do not have the right to purchase sexually explicit entertainment; adults do. Radio and TV broadcasters can be fined for "indecent" programming that children may see or hear; cable and satellite providers can't. The magazine I write for, the *American Prospect*, is published by a tax-exempt educational foundation; even though the *Prospect* exists precisely to comment on politics and government, our editor must be very careful to avoid endorsing any candidate—the tax laws require this. Defenders of *Citizens United* like to note that the expenditure right the Court created in the case also extends to unions. But as we will see below, the Court has had little trouble limiting the right of union leadership to use members' dues and fees for political purposes to protect the rights of dissenters within the ranks. Unions and corporations may both be "persons," but their rights are different.

Even this Supreme Court in January 2012—two years after *Citizens United*—affirmed a lower-court decision that noncitizens do not have the right to engage in "electioneering" in U.S. elections.

That a corporation is a "person" does not mean that its participation in politics has to be completely free of regulation. Any sane system of laws would take into account the facts that bothered Rehnquist: that corporations control vastly more money than individuals; that they never have to "die," and thus can influence events indefinitely; and that, under the most common definitions of corporate governance, they must concern themselves with one thing and one thing only—making profits for their shareholders. Corporations succeed economically precisely because the corporate form of organization makes them more powerful, more resilient, and more dynamic than any individual can be. And the law of free speech, to be anything other than a mockery of democracy, needs to take that imbalance of power into consideration.

Reversing "corporate personhood" won't win the battle against toxic campaign funding. For one thing, corporations aren't the only "persons" taking advantage of the lifting of restrictions on independent expenditures. Nevada casino magnate Sheldon Adelson stepped in to rescue Newt Gingrich's South Carolina campaign with $5 million of his *personal* funds. Any campaign finance reform worth fighting for will need to restrict billionaires as well as billion-dollar corporations.

For another, the Court in *Citizens United* expressly said that it was not relying on the idea of "personhood" to strike down McCain-Feingold's limits on excessive use of money in electioneering. The Court was relying on the nature of the speech itself, not the identity of the speaker. Political speech is the most protected *kind* of speech under the First Amendment. Thus, if by a heroic effort the people somehow enacted a constitutional amendment stating that—in the words of the slogan—"corporations are not people," a future conservative Court would have no trouble striking down limits on corporate political expenditures anyway. Current First Amendment doctrine—dating back nearly fifty years before *Citizens United*—would make the opinion easy to write.

That mention of First Amendment doctrine takes us back to Chief Justice Roberts's improper question: if a state is trying to create a "level playing field," where ordinary citizens' voices are not drowned out by those of the rich, that attempt, to Roberts and his conservative allies, is automatically unconstitutional. Over the past generation, the conservative majorities on the Court have systematically destroyed any idea that the First Amendment relates to democratic self-government, or civic equality.

That problem goes back to the Court's first major campaign-finance decision, *Buckley v. Valeo*, in 1976. *Buckley* considered the campaign-finance reforms that the people had demanded after the disgraceful revelations of the Watergate scandal. In 1972, the Committee to Re-Elect the President (CREEP) mobilized corporate donations around Richard Nixon's reelection campaign. As never before, the White House and the government operated to serve powerful corporate interests and extort campaign contributions from them in return. Underneath the dramatic story of ex-CIA operatives burglarizing Democratic headquarters was the less dramatic but equally shocking story of unaccountable cash "slush funds" in White House safes, with money going directly from donors to political aides to the petty criminals of the White House "Plumbers Unit."

After Nixon's resignation, an outraged public demanded major reform to the campaign finance laws—and Congress complied. The reforms of 1974 limited the total amount of money campaigns could raise and spend, restricted individual contributions to political candidates, set up a public-financing system for presidential elections, restricted so-called independent political expenditures by groups supporting or opposing candidates, and limited the amount of personal funds political candidates could spend for their campaigns. These laws mark a lost opportunity for democratic renewal, and a major progressive victory that—like too many others in American history—was largely neutered by a conservative Court.

In *Buckley*, the Court held that the First Amendment did not allow Congress to restrict the total amount raised and spent by privately financed campaigns, to limit the expenditures of the so-called independent committees, or to restrict the amount a wealthy individual could spend on his or her own political campaign. Although the Court did permit Congress to limit the amount any individual could contribute to a candidate, the net effect of *Buckley* was to negate the effort to make American politics fairer, more open, and less thoroughly dominated by wealthy individuals and corporations.

The Court's reasoning is the same as that inspiring Roberts's improper question from the bench: that *any attempt* to allow the voices of ordinary citizens to be heard as fully as the voices of the wealthy was invalid—on its face. Like Roberts, the majority found the very idea of civic equality to be rank heresy. "[T]he concept that government may restrict the speech of some elements of our society in order to enhance the relative voice of others," the Court's opinion thundered, "is wholly foreign to the First Amendment."[17]

Really? *Wholly* foreign?

Wholly . . . *foreign?*

Is there even a shred of truth in this sentence? Is equality in speech—the right not only to speak but also to be heard—*really* a sinister un-American notion?

The idea does not stand up to serious scrutiny.

Consider, for example, a meeting of your local city council or county board, with an open comment period for citizens to discuss some pending measure. A local organization—let's call it "Citizens United"—signs up to speak first. Then, when its allotted time is up, the organization's representatives simply refuse to give up the microphone to allow others to be heard. Citizens United has more to say, they argue; government cannot "silence" them for the purpose of allowing others to talk. Other citizens are still free: they can shout their comments from the back of the chamber or scribble them on notepaper, fold the pages into paper airplanes, and toss them in the direction of the council members.

Would anyone accept this logic?

Or imagine that Citizens United members come to the meeting with privately purchased bullhorns. After their representative has spoken, they use their bullhorns to drown out speakers who have a different point of view. If the chairman told them to be silent to allow others to speak, would this be "wholly foreign to the First Amendment"? Wouldn't it simply be ordinary democratic procedure, designed to make sure that as many points of view as possible are heard?

The private-bullhorn approach is now the dominant view of free speech. The First Amendment exists, in the new logic, *precisely* to allow those with money to drown out those without. The thrust of much of the

Court's First Amendment jurisprudence in recent years has been to give increased power to the powerful at the expense of the powerless. In a 2007 case, *Federal Election Commission v. Wisconsin Right to Life*, the Court held that an antiabortion group could not be restricted from running ads critical of a pro-choice senator just before he faced reelection. In his opinion, Chief Justice Roberts was characteristically self-righteous: "Where the First Amendment is implicated, the tie goes to the speaker, not the censor," he wrote.[18]

Sounds good. But it turns out that for Roberts and his allies, the tie goes to the speaker only when the speaker is a well-funded organization or institution. Individuals don't fare quite so well. Consider *Morse v. Frederick*, a case decided the same term, again in an opinion by Roberts. In *Morse*, an exuberant high school student stood near his high school when the Olympic Torch was carried past it; as the TV cameras passed over him, he unveiled a banner reading BONG HiTS 4 JESUS. The school principal (or perhaps we should call her for these purposes "the censor") told him to put the banner away; when he refused, the principal suspended him.

Roberts saw no problem with silencing the witless stoner. "BONG HiTS 4 JESUS" *must* have meant—or at least *could* have meant—"bong hits [are a good thing]."[19] Roberts, like school authorities, was shocked (shocked!) to discover that some students think drugs are funny. If students are allowed to say such horrible things, some viewer somewhere *could* conclude that the school somehow agreed with this strange "advocacy" of pot use.

Tie paid the house on that one.

Consider the 2005 case of *Garcetti v. Ceballos*. A deputy Los Angeles County prosecutor found serious defects in a police affidavit that led to a search warrant and a prosecution. When he told his superiors of his view that the warrant was invalid, they ignored him. Defense counsel called him as a witness, and asked him, under oath, about his view of the warrant. When he answered truthfully, his superiors transferred him to a less desirable job and demoted him. He sued, alleging retaliation for exercise of his First Amendment rights. The Court rejected his suit: "[W]hen public employees make statements pursuant to their official duties, the employees are not speaking as citizens for First Amendment purposes, and the Constitution does not insulate their communications from employer discipline."[20]

The house wins again.

As we've seen, schoolchildren can be silenced when they say something that could remotely be interpreted as favoring illegal drugs. Contrast this with the near absolute right of tobacco corporations to urge children of all ages to use *their* addictive drug. In a case called *Lorillard Tobacco v. Reilly,* the Court briskly voided a Massachusetts law forbidding tobacco billboards within one thousand feet of a school. That modest restriction violated Big Tobacco's rights. In fact, the Court went further and held the state could not even protect *toddlers* from addiction propaganda by requiring tobacco advertisements in stores to be posted a minimum of five feet above the floor. Madison would have been appalled, apparently, at such a grave violation of free speech.[21]

So far all the chest-thumping about free speech, this Court is more and more solicitous of the First Amendment rights of corporations and powerful organizations, and, increasingly, openly contemptuous of the predicament of powerless individuals they seek to silence. *Citizens United* was not a radical departure, but simply another way station in the grim transformation of the First Amendment.

Free speech should be—and in the view of those who wrote the First Amendment, would be—an important means by which Americans govern themselves. But in the hands of the Far Right, it has become a major means by which we *are governed* by government and by private forces we cannot answer or even confront.

The result is a slow transformation of our form of government, from republic to corporate oligarchy. The rot has progressed almost to the terminal stage. But remember the words of Miracle Max in *The Princess Bride*: "It just so happens that your friend here is only *mostly* dead. There's a big difference between mostly dead and all dead."[22]

Citizens United has stirred outrage across the board. Corporate shills are complacent—but many citizens, across the political spectrum, are not. Republicans, who were jubilant when the decision came down, spent the spring primary season watching their own presidential field clawing itself to pieces. Each candidate had an "independent" super PAC, free to savage rival candidates, and the result was an unprecedented wave of vicious attack ads against other Republicans.

Even judges are getting into the act. Late last year, the Montana Supreme Court faced a challenge to that state's corporate expenditure laws from a well-funded pro-business group that openly advertised to donors that "if you decide to support this program, no politician, no bureaucrat, and no radical environmentalist will ever know you helped make this program possible."[23]

The Court held that the Supreme Court in *Citizens United* had not considered the unique facts of Montana's long tradition of corporate abuse—outright buying, not just of legislators and elections, but also of actual individual votes. It applied *Citizens United* and upheld Montana's law. "The Supreme Court [in *Citizens United*] held that laws that burden political speech are subject to strict scrutiny, which requires the government to prove that the law furthers a compelling state interest and is narrowly tailored to that interest," the state court noted. "Here the government met that burden."[24]

Montana's rebellion may be crushed. The Supreme Court blocked the Montana court's ruling from taking effect—but it also refused to summarily reverse it. Instead, it has asked for a formal petition for review. In a statement appended to the Court's order, Justice Ruth Bader Ginsburg and Justice Stephen Breyer (both dissenters in *Citizens United*) said, "A petition for certiorari will give the Court an opportunity to consider whether, in light of the huge sums currently deployed to buy candidates' allegiance, *Citizens United* should continue to hold sway."[25]

The Court will hear an earful from parties who are now permitted to file amicus briefs urging the Court to use this case to reverse *Citizens United*. The Court is unlikely to accept that invitation. But, like the nationwide protests and the proposed amendments, the Montana ruling and the amicus briefs will have their effect. If nothing else, it may make the current majority less enthusiastic about extending *Citizens United* to allow direct corporate contributions, or to—as the Far Right eagerly expects them to do—rule that even *disclosure* rules for independent expenditures violate the First Amendment. The Supreme Court likes to feign indifference to public opinion, but sustained opposition by states, other branches of government, and the people can temper the justices' smug certainty.

With luck, we can blunt any move to extend *Citizens United* in the near future; with tenacity, we can reverse this entire line of cases. At this writing, at least a dozen proposed amendments to the Constitution have been introduced in Congress. Cities and counties around the country have passed resolutions protesting the effect the decision has had on their local elections.

Unfortunately, too many of the proposed amendments and protest resolutions focus on the red herring of "corporate personhood." As Kent

Greenfield, a scholar of both corporate and constitutional law, wrote recently, "saying corporations are not persons is as irrelevant to constitutional analysis as saying that [New England Patriots quarterback] Tom Brady does not putt well."[26] Greenfield points out that one problem with current doctrine is that corporate governance currently treats the whims of top management as if they were the interests of shareholders and workers. Contrast those rules with an entirely different set of precedents that protect nonunionized workers in unionized industries against the use of their union agency fees (the amount they pay to the union for representing their interests) for political purposes with which they disagree. When the Obama administration raised the First Amendment rights of shareholders during its consideration of *Citizens United*, the Court brushed the idea aside. "There is . . . little evidence of abuse that cannot be corrected by shareholders 'through the procedures of corporate democracy,'" Justice Kennedy breezily asserted.[27] The Court takes the First Amendment seriously when it limits *union* leadership; corporate leaders are given far more deference.

Anyone who has ever attended a major corporate annual meeting, and any small shareholder who has ever written to a corporation he or she supposedly "owns" part of, would answer Justice Kennedy's question with a question: "What 'corporate democracy' are you talking about?" Most corporate law, however, is state law; state laws protecting shareholder First Amendment interests, and other reforms to corporate law would, then, make "personhood" less of a problem. Advocating for these changes should be part of a progressive response to *Citizens United*.

What we need is advocacy and discussion aimed at reviving the idea of speech as an important component of equality and self-government. Most of the amendments proposed so far don't even mention the idea of "leveling the playing field" or include the most important language—language that would permit the government to institute *mandatory* public finance systems, with no buyout provision for the wealthy, and uniform limitations on "independent" expenditures by corporations *and* wealthy individuals.

Amending the Constitution is a difficult and chancy project. We should undertake it—around an amendment that addresses the real issues of civic equality. A drive to amend the Constitution, if fought intelligently, can be an important mobilizing tool. That's a lesson we learned during the Progressive Era, when communities and ordinary citizens organized around the ideas of popular democracy and economic justice. The success of those efforts is exactly what the current smear campaign against progressives is designed to obliterate.

Whether an amendment is successful or not, however, the fight over the ideas behind *Citizens United* can bear concrete results. For one thing, the Court, in the opinion itself, said that governments can require disclosure of the sources of political money—both for campaign contributions and for corporate and other entities that make "independent" expenditures. Right-wing activists are targeting those next, using the bogus First Amendment argument that doomed Arizona's public-finance system. But we needn't sit by and wait for the Court to decide this issue. If the federal, state, and local governments enact strict disclosure requirements, that will send a counter-message to the Court and to the Far Right—that the people will not sit by quietly while moneyed interests conduct a hostile takeover of our democratic system. In history, the Supreme Court sometimes realizes it has made a mistake and reverses disastrous decisions—think, for example, of *Lawrence v. Texas*, protecting the rights of gay men and lesbians. That decision reversed *Bowers v. Hardwick*, a harshly homophobic decision handed down just seventeen years before.

But even if the Court does not reverse *Citizens United*, American history shows that justices do take into account the popular opposition their decisions stir. A sustained popular movement can, at a minimum, make the far-right majority cautious about extending the precedent, and set the stage for a future Court to rethink the crazy First Amendment logic that has led our jurisprudence down this blind alley.

The struggle will likely be long and difficult. But it is worth waging, both because we can win concrete gains and because it offers progressives an opportunity to change the national dialogue about the First Amendment. Equality and self-government, as ideas in the law, are mostly dead—but not all dead. The battle is not over. Sustained popular pressure may force right-wing courts and activist groups to back off from their continuing demands for special political rights for corporations and the rich. Citizens must unite indeed—around the idea that one-sided, mercenary discourse, not civic equality, is "wholly foreign to the First Amendment."

CHAPTER 6

The Second Amendment Allows Citizens to Threaten Government

"As we go down the rabbit hole of tyranny, at what point are peaceful tactics no longer viable?" a caller asked Representative Ron Paul on a C-SPAN call-in show in 2008. Paul's answer: "You know, the Founders say that you have the Second Amendment because the Second Amendment protects you against the abuse of government—I don't think we are anywhere close to that. But we need to protect the Second Amendment."

Paul invoked the examples of Mohandas Gandhi and Martin Luther King. He then imagined a future "not too far off" in which citizens use their guns against government:

> The tax code is in shambles and is collected in a very uncon-
> stitutional fashion. Already people practice civil disobedience.
> But *boy* is that a personal choice, it's a tough one. The govern-
> ment still has more guns than we have, and therefore you're
> taking on some real serious responsibility. But ultimately
> conditions could get worse where people have to make a tough
> decision on whether or not to practice peaceful civil disobedi-
> ence.[1]

Notice how Paul has managed to lump "peaceful civil disobedience"—peaceful marches, sit-ins, nonviolent boycotts, and public education—with armed resistance to the Internal Revenue Service. Note, too, that in Ron Paul's world, the decision to use weapons is a purely "personal" choice, like Coke or Pepsi. The leaders of the American Revolution did not turn to force before they had petitioned, enlisted their elected officials, and justified their resistance to the world. Not in today's right-wing parlance: those who don't like their tax bills can simply lock and load.

The Far Right has begun to equate free speech and political action—the weapons of Gandhi and King—with bullets. One prominent gun-rights advocate explained the equation this way:

> The Supreme Court has ruled that the First Amendment pro-hibits the government from registering purchasers of newspa-pers and magazines, even of foreign Communist propaganda. The same principle should apply to the Second Amendment: *the tools of political dissent should be privately owned and un-registered.*[2]

Few figures in American history—and increasingly, around the world—are more revered than that of the lone protester resisting tyranny in the name of freedom and democracy. Paul cited Gandhi and King, knowing that listeners of all political persuasions accept these figures—radical for their time—as symbols of morality and the democratic impulse. But pro-gun extremists in the United States have begun yet another piece of dishonest historical revisionism. They are airbrushing assault weapons into these remembered scenes of civic heroism. The new protester doesn't use "soul force" to convert enemies with the power of reason and love; he points weapons at them and, if he personally chooses, blows them away. It's particularly shameful when you consider that both Gandhi and King, after years of speaking out for peace, nonviolence, and self-government, were killed by fanatics with firearms.

Like his father, Rand Paul also likes to hint that the remedy for rejec-tion of his libertarian policies may be hot lead. *Death and Taxes* magazine quotes him as saying, "Some citizens are holding out hope that the up-coming elections will better things. We'll wait and see. Lots of us believe that maybe that's an unreliable [method] considering that the Fabian progressive socialists have been chipping at our foundations for well over 100 years. Regardless, the founders made sure we had Plan B: the Second Amendment."[3] During the same election cycle, Tea Party–backed Senate candidate Sharron Angle warned that if she was unable to defeat Demo-cratic senator Harry Reid at the ballot box (she couldn't), citizens would turn to "Second Amendment remedies"—in essence, assassination.[4]

America today faces a gun crisis. While the overall crime rate has fallen since 1990, one number remains stubbornly high—the number of mass shootings by deranged individuals. We have seen them in recent years at workplaces, in private homes, in colleges and universities, and in high schools. In January 2011, a mentally ill man, who had been able to buy weapons with no restriction, showed up at a "Congress on the Corner" civic event in Tucson, Arizona. He opened fire, killing Federal Judge John Roll and five others, and wounding fourteen, including Representative Gabrielle Giffords, who was hurt so badly that she was forced to resign her seat a year later. There seemed to be little political purpose behind the shooter's act. But the act of taking a gun to a peaceful meeting with a lawmaker evoked the stunning sight, in 2010, of right-wing activists carrying guns to congressional "town meetings"—and even, on one occasion, to an appearance by President Obama.

In 2008, the Supreme Court recognized—for the first time in American history—the "right to bear arms" as a personal, individual right, permitting law-abiding citizens to possess handguns in their home for their personal protection. Two years later, it held that both state and federal governments must observe this newly recognized right. These decisions— *District of Columbia v. Heller*[5] and *McDonald v. City of Chicago*[6]—represented a huge pro-gun shift in constitutional law. A leading conservative judge, J. Harvie Wilkinson III of the Court of Appeals for the Fourth Circuit, found the *Heller* decision so radical that he publicly compared it to every conservative's most hated decision, *Roe v. Wade.*[7]

Curiously enough, the Far Right responded to these victories—which seemed unthinkable only a few years earlier—as if the sky had fallen. During Senate consideration of the nomination of Elena Kagan to the Supreme Court, Senator Jeff Sessions of Alabama direly warned that the two gun cases were 5–4 decisions. "Most Americans are totally unaware [that] the Second Amendment hangs by a mere thread," he said.[8]

They're not aware of this chiefly because it isn't true. The idea that the rights of ordinary gun owners are in danger is a fallacy. But it is being spread for specific political reasons. Republican hacks like Sessions know that it is bad politics to tell the truth, which is that the advocates of the Second Amendment have recently won an unprecedented victory. The Second Amendment right to own firearms for hunting and self-protection is now virtually unquestioned in our law and politics. Even candidate Barack

Obama endorsed the Supreme Court decision in *Heller*. But politicians and right-wing fund-raisers need credulous pro-gun voters to rush to the polls in terror that some sinister force (remember Lester Pearce's warnings about blue-helmeted U.N. troops on the streets of Phoenix?) is on the very verge of seizing their guns.

Beyond that, the Far Right is seeking to disable any commonsense limitation on weapons ownership. They have already won a statute permitting gun owners to take their guns into national parks. The Second Amendment, they now argue, forbids any laws against carrying of concealed weapons, even in restaurants, bars, or college classrooms. It bars laws against gun ownership by domestic abusers and felons. It forbids restrictions even on automatic weapons, bazookas, and grenades. Virginia attorney general Ken Cuccinelli, a far-right darling, recently issued an opinion stating that the right to bear arms invalidated even a state law banning guns from places of worship.[9] These extremists—who in other contexts like to blather about "states' rights"—also want a federal statute overriding the gun permit and registration laws of states that have not bought into their agenda. A holder of a gun permit in a state like Arizona would thus have a federal statutory right to carry a concealed weapon in a state like New York, where laws are more restrictive.

A society that can't regulate guns at all will soon degenerate into violent anarchy. Why would the Constitution guarantee unrestricted access to the means of mass violence? This is where the idea that shooting people is Gandhi-King-style dissent comes into play. It is what authors Joshua Horwitz and Casey Anderson call "the insurrectionist idea." Extremists claim that the Founders wrote the Second Amendment because freedom can only be protected by an armed citizenry able to threaten tax collectors or other meddling officials with instant death.

As UCLA law professor Adam Winkler writes in his recent book, *Gunfight: The Battle over the Right to Bear Arms in America*,

> [The] radical wing of the gun rights movement focuses less on the value of guns for self-defense against criminals than on their value for fighting tyranny. They argue that guns are the last line of defense against our government, which is determined to deprive Americans of their rights. The Second Amendment, in this view, gives Americans the right to rise up and revolt against the government. It guarantees, in other words, not only a right to bear arms but a right of insurrection.[10]

Insurrectionists claim that their agenda is yet another campaign to "restore" the "original meaning" of the Constitution. Their evidence for that is scant, but they often cite this quotation from Thomas Jefferson, America's third president:

> When governments fear the people, there is liberty. When the people fear the government, there is tyranny. The strongest reason for the people to retain the right to keep and bear arms is, as a last resort, to protect themselves against tyranny in government.[11]

That one is an argument ender. Who could argue with Jefferson? Well, not me, to be sure. But there's a problem with this quote, as there is with so much of the phony history and overheated rhetoric about the Second Amendment.

It's bogus.

As far as scholars can tell, Jefferson never said it. Monticello.org, the official website of the Thomas Jefferson Foundation, says, "We have not found any evidence that Thomas Jefferson said or wrote, 'When governments fear the people, there is liberty. When the people fear the government, there is tyranny,' or any of its listed variations."[12] The quotation (which has also been misattributed to revolutionary leader Samuel Adams, Thomas Paine, and *The Federalist*) actually *was* written (as his own work) in 1914 by an obscure radical political thinker named John Basil Barnhill, during a published debate in a socialist magazine called the *National Rip-Saw*.[13]

Just as bogus as the quote is the idea behind it: that the purpose of the Second Amendment was to create a citizenry able to intimidate the government, and that America will be a better place if government officials live in constant fear of gun violence. If good government actually came from a violent, armed population, then Somalia would be the best-governed place on earth. As we saw from the 2010 shootings of Roll and Giffords, the consequences for democracy of guns in private hands without reasonable regulation can be dire—a society where a member of Congress cannot meet constituents without suffering traumatic brain injury, and where a federal judge cannot stop by a meeting on his way back from Mass without being shot dead.

The history and meaning of the Second Amendment are complicated subjects. Scholars have spilled oceans of ink interpreting its complicated wording and the ideas behind it. A fair reading of the entire text of the Constitution suggests to me that the most prominent concern of its framers was protecting states' control of their militias. That's not to say that there was no personal aspect of the "right to bear arms," but state militias, and militia service, were its primary concern.

Under Article I § 8 of the Constitution, the states transferred to Congress the power "to provide for calling forth the militia to execute the laws of the union, suppress insurrections and repel Invasions" and "to provide for organizing, arming, and disciplining, the militia." This was one of the most radical features of the original Constitution. Under the Articles of Confederation, states had complete control of their militias. Opponents of ratification feared that the new federal government would dissolve the state militias and use its new power to raise and support armies to create a federal military that would rule the country by force.

The Second Amendment's text most clearly addressed that concern: it promises that the state militias will not be disarmed by the central government. That background has led a number of historians to suggest that the amendment has no real relation to any personal right of individuals to "keep and bear arms." For much of American history, the Court seemed to assume that protecting state militias was the main purpose of the amendment and that personal gun possession was not guaranteed.

History is rarely that clear, however. The notion of personal gun possession as a right is also deeply rooted in American history and, before that, in English law. *Gunfight* author Winkler notes that since before the amendment was proposed, many citizens have discussed the right to bear arms as a guarantee against tyranny as well as a feature of a federal system. But the protection against tyranny was a long-term structural guarantee, not a privilege of individual nullification, he said in an interview: "I don't think there's any support for the idea that government officials should be afraid of being shot." [14]

In fact, Winkler's book makes clear that throughout American history, no one—including no less a conservative icon than Ronald Reagan when he was governor of California—has seriously questioned that the government can enact reasonable regulation of citizens' use of weapons. Certainly the Founders did not. "The founders believed that ordinary people should have guns and that government shouldn't be allowed to completely disarm the citizenry," he writes. "Yet their vision was certainly not that of today's gun rights hard-liners, who dismiss nearly any gun regulation as an infringement on individual liberty. . . . They might not have termed it 'gun control,' but the founders understood that gun rights had to be balanced with public safety needs."[15]

The "insurrection" idea stems from the mid-1970s, when far-right extremists took over national gun-owner groups like the National Rifle Association and began to use them as mouthpieces for their antigovernment philosophy. That sharp turn to the right has driven a wedge between the NRA and many law-enforcement groups, whose members understand that police are the first casualties of crazed "insurrection." It also calls into question the groups' right to speak for the millions of law-abiding gun owners they claim to represent.

The history behind the insurrection idea is scant. It would be odd indeed if the framers of the Constitution and the Bill of Rights had written an amendment designed to give individuals the right to liquidate the government they were setting up. When they gathered in Philadelphia in 1787, the original framers were acutely aware that armed bands of farmers in Massachusetts had revolted against the state government only a few months earlier. George Washington, in particular, found the news of Daniel Shays's rebellion in that state so disturbing that it contributed to his decision to come out of retirement and help frame a new national charter that would allow a central government to suppress local rebellions.

At Philadelphia, Gouverneur Morris warned the delegates that failure to create a national government would precipitate new outbreaks of rebellion and, eventually, civil war. "The scenes of horror attending civil commotion can not be described, and the conclusion of them will be worse than the term of their continuance," he said. "The stronger party will then make traytors of the weaker; and the gallows & halter will finish the work of the sword."[16]

After becoming president, Washington personally led a national army into western Pennsylvania to suppress a rebellion against the new federal tax on whiskey. Invoking the spirit of 1776, the "whiskey rebels" had tarred and feathered a federal tax collector, then held protest meetings where they threatened revolution. Washington was furious. In response, he marched with the army to Pennsylvania—the only time in American history a president has served as commander-in-chief *in the field*. In a subsequent message to Congress, he showed precious little sympathy for insurrectionary "Second Amendment remedies":

> [T]o yield to the treasonable fury of so small a portion of the United States, would be to violate the fundamental principle of our constitution, which enjoins that the will of the majority shall prevail. . . . [S]ucceeding intelligence has tended to manifest the necessity of what has been done; it being now confessed by those who were not inclined to exaggerate the ill-conduct of the insurgents, that their malevolence was not pointed merely to a particular law; but that a spirit, inimical to all order, has actuated many of the offenders.[17]

In the *McDonald* decision, the Supreme Court held that the personal "right to bear arms" is one of the fundamental rights incorporated in the Fourteenth Amendment and, through it, applied to the states as well as the federal government. When the Fourteenth Amendment was framed, the former Confederate states were enacting laws to prevent newly freed slaves from having weapons. Some of the framers of the amendment expressed concern that this would leave Southern black people defenseless against white vigilantes, and that it violated their Second Amendment rights. Yale scholar Akhil Reed Amar explains that in the debate over the Fourteenth Amendment, "Reconstruction Republicans recast arms bearing as a core *civil* right, utterly divorced from the militia and other political rights and responsibilities. Arms were needed not as part of political and politicized militia service but to protect one's individual homestead."[18]

The right to protect the homestead, however, isn't the right to shoot down government officials. And it is most emphatically not the right to form armed gangs and give them high-sounding "militia" names. In fact, the framers of the Fourteenth Amendment were concerned about armed gangs with guns—violent white-supremacist rebels who were, let's face it, the spiritual ancestors of some of the "insurrectionists" of today. These terrorists—called the Ku Klux Klan, the "Night Riders," or the Knights of the White Camellia—were terrorizing and killing newly free citizens who sought to participate in Southern society. Like the armed thugs at congressional town hall meetings, they sought to control democratic politics with terror. In the South, the hooded-terrorist side already had guns. Personal protection, not rebellion, was the object of "incorporation." And personal protection, not rebellion, is the focus of the Second Amendment right recognized in *Heller* and *McDonald*.

In 2011, as in the 1790s and as in Southern Reconstruction, there is abroad in the land "a spirit, inimical to all order," particularly if that order concerns federally guaranteed environmental protection, economic regulation, or civil rights. In January 2011, anonymous thugs entered Missouri legislative office buildings and placed red bull's-eye stickers near the offices of Democratic lawmakers who support the Affordable Care Act.[19] In 2010, Tea Party activists in Virginia posted what they thought was the home address of Representative Tom Perriello (D-VA), an outspoken supporter of health care reform. The website suggested that self-styled patriots "drop by" and "express their thanks." Actually, the address was the home of Perriello's brother, Bo, and his family. That day, someone went to Bo Perriello's house and cut the gas line. That might have caused an explosion and even killed the people inside. One of the activists who posted the incorrect address at first dismissed the incident as "collateral damage."[20] He later apologized, but that first reaction is a good example of "insurrectionist" thinking. "Patriots" are at war with government, and if innocent people are terrorized or harmed, well, that's war.

The danger and intimidation aren't focused only on Democrats or progressives. In early 2010, someone fired a shot at the office of no less staunch a conservative than Representative Eric Cantor (R-VA), who is Jewish.[21] Police later concluded that the shots were "random," but no one who heard the news could at first help suspecting an act of anti-Semitic violence. Increasingly, when we confront the political divisions among Americans, we find ourselves wondering about physical danger and gunshots. Members of Congress, who not long ago mixed freely with their constituents, are now thinking carefully about bodyguards and body armor. An open, democratic system can't survive amid constant fear of political murder.

Voices from the Far Right are trying to plant a parasitic meme in our Bill of Rights: that America is not a self-governing republic, but a dark Hobbesian plane where each "sovereign citizen" chooses what laws to obey, and any census taker or federal law-enforcement agent had better beware. The long-term result of such a "right to bear arms" would be an ungovernable state of nature, where life, both civic and individual, would be solitary, poor, nasty, brutish, and short.

The Second Amendment now securely protects a right to personal self-defense. But that right is to self-defense against assault, not immunity from the law. The existence of a right doesn't protect its holders against all regulation. Free speech doesn't guarantee my right to block traffic with rallies; or to enter private property, like a church, and disrupt services with a speech; or to stand outside private homes with a bullhorn and berate the people who live there. The Second Amendment shouldn't entitle me to carry a gun to church or into government buildings or schools. It shouldn't entitle me to own a machine gun, much less armor-piercing ammunition.

Commonsense concern with the consequences of legal rules, not chest thumping about squirrel rifles and the Revolutionary War, will produce a system of laws that recognizes the nation's heritage of gun ownership and also protects us all from Somalia-style chaos.

CHAPTER 7

The Tenth Amendment Protects "States' Rights" and "State Sovereignty"

On April 15, 2009, Governor Rick Perry of Texas addressed a Tea Party rally in Austin. His fiery anti-Washington remarks were greeted by chants of "Secede! Secede!" Afterward, the governor tried to reassure reporters that he doesn't actually want to break up the Union—not yet, anyway. "Texas is part of a great Union, and I see no reason for that to change," he said. But then he added, "When we came into the Union in 1845, one of the issues was that we would be able to leave if we decided to do that. My hope is that America, and Washington in particular, pay attention. We've got a great Union. There's absolutely no reason to dissolve it. But if Washington continues to thumb their nose at the American people, who knows what may come of that?"[1]

Perry's affable threat of civil war came a week after he affirmed his support for a resolution in the Texas Legislature in which the state would "claim sovereignty under the Tenth Amendment to the Constitution of the United States over all powers not otherwise enumerated and granted to the federal government of the United States." The resolution would have served "as notice and demand to the federal government, as our agent, to cease and desist, effective immediately, mandates that are beyond the scope of these constitutionally delegated powers."[2]

As it happened, the bill never passed. Texas's legislature possessed better sense than its governor. But the bill was a part of a larger movement in which nearly a dozen states have now passed similar resolutions "reclaiming" their "sovereignty" under the Tenth Amendment and generally telling the U.S. government to do what the state legislatures want or face . . . well . . . like . . . you know . . . totally cheesed-off state legislatures.[3]

By itself, this entire thing would be no more than the kind of show-boat shenanigans that make any state capital a fun place to hang out, no more harmful than a bill to designate May as National Axolotl Month. But there's an added fillip: The "sovereignty resolutions" are part of an extremist movement designed to convince the American people that state legislatures and governors have the "right" not only to oppose but also to "nullify" federal laws of which they don't approve.

When states begin to claim the right to override federal law, the national dialogue has entered the beating heart of Crazy Town. The idea of "nullification" directly contradicts the history, text, and structure of the real Constitution, with its insistence on federal supremacy—a federal statute, according to Article VI § 2, is "the supreme law of the land . . . any thing in the constitution or laws of any state to the contrary notwithstanding." And there's a painful history here: this crackpot notion has on several occasions brought the nation to, or over, the brink of civil violence. Its reappearance is a direct assault on our democratic system.

As Perry's remarks illustrate, the movement is being used by ambitious politicians seeking a temporary advantage. (Perry's nullification and secession antics were part of a move to defeat a primary challenge from Senator Kay Bailey Hutchinson.) But it has been generated by a group of far-right radicals who deny every fact of American history and misrepresent the text of the Constitution. They claim that the Tenth Amendment preserves the "sovereignty" and "rights" of the states and restricts the federal government to acting in a few areas. The great mass of federal legislation, including virtually all economic regulations, violates this mighty amendment, they claim.

What is this about? Does the Tenth Amendment give states a veto over federal legislation?

No.

Ian Millhiser of the Center for American Progress has dubbed these dangerous crackpots "Tenthers." Their phony "constitutionalism" is as bogus as the claims that Barack Obama was born in Kenya.[4] The "birther" movement was crippled when Obama produced his long-form birth certificate from Hawaii. A study of the birth documents of the United States should do the same for the "Tenther" movement.

What do "Tenthers" claim? Senator Jim DeMint last year phrased it this way: "The Tenth Amendment says powers not explicitly given to the federal government in the Constitution go to the states or to the people."[5] Rick Perry hails "the spirit and intent of the Tenth Amendment—that all powers not specifically granted to the federal government are reserved to the states and to the people."[6] Mitt Romney, who often plays a conservative on television, carefully hedged his inner Perry during a speech at the Iowa State Fair: "I believe in the Constitution as it was framed by the founders. By the way, I like all the amendments, not just a few of them. Those who served in state government are particularly fond of the 10th amendment. Those that don't know it, I will give you the top line. The 10th amendment says roughly this, it says that those powers not *specifically* granted to the federal government are to be reserved by the states and the people."[7]

Are they right? Let's look at the text, which reads, in its entirety: "The powers not delegated to the United States by the Constitution, nor prohibited by it to the States, are reserved to the States respectively, or to the people."

Notice that DeMint and Perry, like a lot of "Tenthers," managed to sneak words into the text that the framers didn't write. The words are "explicitly" (DeMint) or "specifically" (Perry). Neither is there. (Romney apparently knows the words aren't there and wants to sound like a "Tenther" without actually lying—hence the Romneyesque "roughly.")

Nothing in the Tenth Amendment says that the powers must be *explicitly, expressly,* or *specifically* given to the federal government—given, that is, in so many words. Also note that the amendment doesn't mention state "sovereignty"; in fact, that idea appears nowhere in the Constitution. Nor does the Tenth Amendment (or the rest of the Constitution) mention "rights" for the states. Finally, there's nothing in it about state "nullification" of federal law.

Does the amendment really, in Da Vinci Code fashion, include those ideas? Compare the language of the Articles of Confederation: "Each state retains its *sovereignty,* freedom, and independence, and every power, jurisdiction, and *right,* which is not by this confederation *expressly* delegated to the United States, in Congress assembled."

When the First Congress revised this measure to draft the Tenth Amendment, Perry's and DeMint's words didn't make the cut. The Articles were familiar to every member of the First Congress. Did they just run out of ink?

Since the amendment was adopted, constitutional thinkers have concluded that the *express* powers delegated to the federal government by the Constitution necessarily carry with them the *implied* powers needed to carry them out. That conclusion is bolstered by the sweeping language of the Necessary and Proper Clause, which gives Congress power "to make all laws which shall be necessary and proper for carrying into execution the foregoing powers, and all other powers vested by this Constitution in the government of the United States, or in any department or officer thereof."

If "implied powers" still sounds like tricky lawyer talk, ask yourself the following question: Is the American flag unconstitutional? The Constitution doesn't make any reference to a national flag. By the "express" argument, states and *only* states would retain what we might call "the flag power." The U.S. Army would have to march under the fifty state flags, depending on the origin of each unit. That would be cumbersome, confusing, and dangerous—and more to the point, stupid. Congress can "raise and support armies." Armies have to have flags—they are required under international law and necessary for military discipline and cohesion. A country that has an explicit power to raise an army has the *implied* power to designate a flag. Nobody seriously reads a constitution any other way.

Conservatives certainly don't read it that way when there's a power they want the government to have. (In fact, one pundit at the Tenth Amendment Center recently replied to my "flag" argument by suggesting that of course there can be a *flag*, just not *other things* not explicitly mentioned: "So yes Mr. Epps, the feds can commission a flag. Create a national health care system not so much."[8] Why? Voices in the head apparently told the author so.)

James Madison didn't read the Tenth Amendment that way either. Madison was the sponsor of the proposed Bill of Rights in Congress. It's important to understand Madison's motives in bringing the draft Bill of Rights into the First Congress. The framers of the Constitution, being fallible, had committed a serious tactical error in writing the original document. By the end of the summer of 1787, after settling questions about the structure and powers of the federal government, they were too tired and grouchy to spend weeks more creating a Bill of Rights.

But when the Constitution moved to the states for ratification, many Americans cried foul. The framers lamely tried to claim that a Bill of

Rights wasn't needed. Constitutional historian Leonard Levy expresses the historical consensus about this argument: "That the Framers of the Constitution actually believed their own arguments to justify the omission of a bill of rights is difficult to credit."[9] The people didn't credit it either. They wanted a strong government, but they wanted strong individual rights as well.

Eventually a number of states ratified, but the omission of a Bill of Rights came within a whisker of defeating the Constitution. A number of state resolutions of ratification included a demand for a Bill of Rights. This popular movement created an opportunity for enemies of a powerful national government, such as Virginia's Patrick Henry. They were agitating in the states for a new Constitutional Convention to frame a Bill of Rights—one that would write "states' rights" and "state sovereignty" into the text and gut the strong federal government the framers had worked so hard to create.

Madison stymied them by proposing his own Bill of Rights in Congress. If you read the first ten amendments that actually passed, you'll be struck by their relentless focus on *individual*, not state, rights. Madison's amendments preserve the supremacy of the federal government. The Tenth Amendment was his only nod to the question of how much state authority the new Constitution left intact. It carefully didn't limit the federal government to "explicit" powers, as the Articles had.

This question was specifically discussed during the brief congressional debates on the Bill of Rights. When Representative Thomas Tucker of South Carolina moved to insert the word "expressly" into what became the Tenth Amendment, Madison (in an eyewitness account reprinted in *The Complete Bill of Rights*, edited by Neil Cogan) "[o]bjected to this amendment, because it was impossible to confine a government to the exercise of express powers, there must necessarily be admitted powers by implication, unless the constitution descended to recount every minutiae. He [Madison] remembered the word 'expressly' had been moved in the convention of Virginia, by the opponents to the ratification, and after full and fair discussion was given up by them, and the system allowed to retain its present form."[10] Tucker's amendment never made it into the text.

In order to smuggle the words *explicitly* or *expressly* back into the Constitution, De Mint and Perry have to engage in "everybody knows" originalism. So the framers left out one word? So what? To quote Rick Perry, "Oops." "Everybody knows" they were *thinking* it.

"Everybody" didn't include Madison; nor did it include Chief Justice John Marshall. As chief justice, he first interpreted the amendment for the Supreme Court. He found the omission significant. In *McCulloch v. Maryland*, Marshall rejected the argument that because Congress had no *express* power to create a bank, it was *forbidden* to do so. The power to create a bank was implied by the Commerce Power and other powers over the creation of money and the collection of taxes, he said. He noted the absence of "expressly" in the Tenth Amendment: "The men who drew and adopted this amendment had experienced the embarrassments resulting from the insertion of this word in the Articles of Confederation, and probably omitted it to avoid those embarrassments."[11]

As for "nullification," it has a sinister history. As we've seen, the idea of a state "nullifying" a federal law, and blocking its enforcement, flies directly in the face of the Constitution's text. Advocates like to claim that Jefferson and Madison created the idea when, in 1798, they led the Republican opposition to the Alien and Sedition Acts. Both men believed that the Acts were unconstitutional because they violated the First Amendment. Jefferson wrote a draft resolution for the Kentucky Legislature in which he suggested that "where powers are assumed which have not been delegated, a nullification of the act is the rightful remedy."[12]

As historian Gordon Wood notes, however, "fortunately for his subsequent reputation, the Kentucky legislature edited out this inflammatory term."[13] Wood notes that Madison disagreed with the idea that legislatures could block federal law; Madison "seems to have thought of his resolutions as protests rather than acts of nullification."[14] In Madison's corresponding Virginia Resolution, the legislature contented itself with "declaring" that "the acts aforesaid are unconstitutional."[15] No hint of nullification there; it's limited to political protest—which every state legislature has a right to engage in.

Nullification in the sense that today's "Tenthers" use the term is actually the brainchild of John C. Calhoun, the greatest defender American slavery ever had. When Congress passed a tariff that mildly harmed South Carolina's slave economy, Calhoun and his allies called a "Nullification Convention," and in 1832 this rump body "nullified" the tariff and warned that any attempt to collect it "shall not be lawful."[16]

Madison, living in retirement, was appalled. The ideas of 1798 had been "perverted," he wrote, adding, "It is remarkable how closely the nullifiers who make the name of Mr. Jefferson the pedestal for their colossal heresy, shut their eyes and lips, whenever his authority is ever so clearly and emphatically against them. . . . One thing at least seems to be too clear to be questioned; that whilst a State remains within the Union it cannot withdraw its citizens from the operation of the Constitution & laws of the Union."[17]

In the White House was Andrew Jackson, probably the strongest "states' rights" president in American history. Jackson saw "nullification" for the dangerous fraud it is. "Do not be deceived by names," he said in a message to the country. "Disunion by armed force is *treason*." Jackson offered to support negotiations in Congress to reform the tariff legally. In the meantime, though, he sent reinforcements to federal garrisons and armed ships to Charleston harbor. He privately warned South Carolina leaders that "if one drop of blood be shed there in defiance of the laws of the United States, I will hang the first man of them I can get my hands on to the first tree I can find."[18]

His firmness worked; no other state responded to South Carolina's call. The tariff crisis was resolved the way the framers would have intended—through political negotiations between state officials, members of Congress, and the White House.

Thirty years later, the Civil War interred the idea that the states had the "right" to defy federal law; nearly a million people died, and so did the doctrines of Calhoun. "Nullification" didn't reappear until the 1950s, when Southern segregationist editor James J. Kilpatrick—the Rush Limbaugh of his time—revived the idea as a strategy for blocking school integration. "Only if the citizens of Virginia, as Virginians; or of Texas, as Texans; or of Iowa, as Iowans, insist upon a strict obedience to the spirit of the Tenth Amendment, can the Federal juggernaut be slowed," he warned.[19] The tactic for slowing it was for state legislatures to "nullify" *Brown v. Board* and block any attempt at desegregation by closing down the public schools.

This doctrine, too, met an ignominious death when presidents Eisenhower and Kennedy sent federal troops into defiant Southern states to enforce desegregation orders. But the idea of nullification, like the faint scent of honeysuckle, lingers in the imagination of the neo-Confederate Far Right, and emerges to mislead inexperienced legislators into believing that if they just clap their hands, the Tinker Bell of "state sovereignty" won't die.

The best way to read the Tenth Amendment we actually have is that its words mean what they say, and not what they don't say. The Constitution grants Congress full powers over the objects laid out in Article I § 8, and all the implied powers "necessary and proper" to using its enumerated powers. Under Article VI § 2, federal law is supreme, "any thing," including even high-sounding resolutions of "nullification" drawn up in fringe-right think tanks, "in the constitution or laws of any state to the contrary notwithstanding."

Of course the Constitution guarantees a role for the states. Some powers are given exclusively to the federal government and cannot be shared, such as the power to conduct war and negotiate peace, regulate currency and emit bills of credit, or set the discipline of the armed forces and state militias. Some powers are given to the states, and can't be taken by the federal government, including the power to designate state capitals, adopt state constitutions, draw the political boundaries of cities and towns, choose the officers of their state militias, direct the actions of state officials, and enact state laws.

Many powers are explicitly *denied* to the states—for example, they can't negotiate agreements *even among themselves* without Congress's permission. Some are expressly *denied* to the federal government—the power to require the trial of a federal crime to take place in a state where the crimes did not occur, for example.

The rest—the powers that aren't given explicitly and exclusively to one government or the other—belong to *the people*. The people are the holders of "rights"; they are the holders of "sovereignty." And, being sovereign, the people can insist that powers be *shared* by the states and the federal government, relying on the political process and on their own supremacy as expressed in presidential and congressional election, to police the federal-state boundaries. That's the role of political negotiation and elections.

Throughout American history, the restrictive reading of the Tenth Amendment, and the allied doctrines of "state sovereignty" and "nullification," have been associated with the defense of slavery and segregation. Today, for the moment, those causes have been vanquished. But "Tenthers" still display a hankering for a world in which the lower orders knew their place and the federal government couldn't intrude. Consider a practice that is closer to slavery than most of us want our country to get: child labor in mines and factories.

Not long before he was sworn in as a new member of the Senate, Tea Party favorite Mike Lee (R-UT) gave a speech in Draper, Utah, about the horrors of federal legislation in the Progressive Era. Lee is a strong "Tenther" and a proponent of state "nullification" of the Affordable Care Act. Here's what he said about child labor:

> Congress decided it wanted to prohibit [child labor], so it passed a law—no more child labor. The Supreme Court heard a challenge to that and the Supreme Court decided a case in 1918 called *Hammer v. Dagenhart.* In that case, the Supreme Court acknowledged something very interesting—that, as reprehensible as child labor is, and as much as it ought to be abandoned—that's something that has to be done by state legislators, not by Members of Congress. . . .
>
> This may sound harsh, but it was designed to be that way. It was designed to be a little bit harsh. Not because we like harshness for the sake of harshness, but because we like a clean division of power, so that everybody understands whose job it is to regulate what.
>
> Now, we got rid of child labor, notwithstanding this case. So the entire world did not implode as a result of that ruling.[20]

In his remarks on child labor, Lee did not mention a couple of things. The first is that the federal law did not simply say "no more child labor." The Keating-Owen Child Labor Act of 1916 was actually very carefully drawn to respect the contours of the Constitution's grant to the Congress of the power to "regulate commerce with foreign nations, and among the several states, and with the Indian tribes." It forbade businesses to "ship or deliver for shipment in interstate or foreign commerce, any article or commodity" produced with child labor.[21] And the Keating-Owen Act was not the product of a spoiled Congress banning child labor on a pettish whim; it was the culmination of decades of sustained, informed national demand by the people—sovereigns in our system—that American commerce be cleansed of this barbaric relic of the past.

Second, the only reason "we got rid of child labor, notwithstanding this case," was that in 1938—after two needless additional decades of what Justice Holmes correctly called "ruined lives"—the Supreme Court overruled *Hammer v. Dagenhart* and held that the federal government *can* bar the products of child labor and other unfair labor practices from interstate commerce.[22] Had it not done so, it's pretty clear that children in (you fill in the state) would be suffocating in mines and factories today. If you doubt that, consider that the Fair Labor Standards Act's child-labor provisions don't apply to use of children as "hand harvest laborer[s]" in agriculture.[23] According to a 2010 Human Rights Watch report, "Hundreds of thousands of children under age 18 are working in agriculture in the United States."[24]

The third thing Lee did not mention is that nothing actually in the Constitution says that regulation of shipment of child-produced goods in interstate commerce "has to be done by state legislators, not by Members of Congress." The Tenth Amendment sure doesn't say it. This is "voices in the head" originalism at its worst. Lee cannot point to anything in the text of the Constitution that "was designed to be a little bit harsh." Like the "Tenther" voices he hears, the harshness is in his head.

CHAPTER 8

The Fourteenth Amendment Is Obsolete and Irrelevant

Arizona state senator Russell Pearce is the author of a measure designed to punish American-born children who have the bad taste to grow in the womb of an illegal alien. (He's also the brother of Lester Pearce, the Arizona justice of the peace who was my instructor in the far-right "meaning" of the Constitution.) Russell Pearce's proposed statute would allow the state to decide which children born in Arizona are U.S. citizens, and to give special second-class birth certificates to babies whose parents can't prove their immigration status.

This statute flew directly in the face of the Constitution's text. The Fourteenth Amendment's Citizenship Clause says, "All persons born or naturalized in the United States, and subject to the jurisdiction thereof, are citizens of the United States and of the State wherein they reside." The language seems pretty clear: children of illegal aliens are born in the United States, and they are subject to U.S. law. That doesn't matter, Pearce said. The Fourteenth Amendment's citizenship clause was written only to apply to blacks.

"When the Fourteenth Amendment was written, it was written to give credit to the African Americans, recognize them," Pearce told CNN in 2010. And anyway, the framers of the Fourteenth Amendment wrote it wrong. The amendment "was written by the same Congress that wrote the Civil Rights [Act] of 1866 . . . that has similar language that makes it very clear [that children of illegal aliens were not citizens], and they should have used that same language [in the Fourteenth Amendment]," he said.[1]

103

Pearce is perhaps America's leading proponent of a systematic attack on American-born children of undocumented aliens. He's hardly a constitutional authority, though. In his CNN appearance, he misquoted the framing debates of the Fourteenth Amendment, cited Supreme Court cases by the wrong names, and gave inaccurate summaries of their holdings. Even in Arizona, the Mississippi of the twenty-first century, where anti-immigrant feeling has been fanned to white heat by right-wing zealots, Pearce ended up going too far: in November 2011, his constituents made him the first Arizona state legislator in history to be bounced from office in a recall election.

The important moment in his CNN appearance is when Pearce corrects the Constitution: *"they should have used that same language,"* those stupid framers. This is Da Vinci Code originalism at its most dangerous. Pearce didn't make it up all by himself—it is coming from anti-immigration advocates and scholars at the very far right edge of American politics. It is being used nationwide in a campaign to strip the Citizenship Clause of the meaning embodied in both its history and text.

And this attack concerns only the first sentence of the Fourteenth Amendment. Pearce's wrong-headed analysis highlights a problem that pervades far-right "constitutionalism": while they endlessly swear fidelity to the Constitution, they are eager to make one of its most important provisions disappear.

Harvard scholars Theda Skocpol and Vanessa Williamson provide a stark illustration of this selective reverence. In their book, *The Tea Party and the Remaking of Republican Conservatism*, they introduce readers to Jerry DeLemus, a Tea Party leader in New Hampshire. DeLemus reveres the Constitution so deeply that at his home, family dinner begins with a reading from the Bible coupled with a reading from the Constitution. But the Constitution reading seems to be selective. At a meeting of a local "constitutionalist" group, the authors record, "Jerry DeLemus mentioned that he might prefer to limit the amendments to the Constitution to the first ten, those in the Bill of Rights, omitting the rest of it altogether."[2]

Selective far-right readers are particularly eager to make the Fourteenth Amendment disappear. To understand the danger in this delusion, we have to grasp the central role that amendment plays in our democratic society.

The Constitution we live under has been amended twenty-seven times since 1787. In combination, those amendments have changed our system of government into something the Philadelphia framers would not recognize: a modern democracy.

That's good: that's what Article V is for.

Of those twenty-seven amendments, none is more important than the Fourteenth. It changed virtually everything about the republic designed at Philadelphia—for the better. Progressives who criticize the Constitution because many framers were elitist and pro-slavery are not fully dealing with the Fourteenth Amendment, which was designed to wipe those stains out of the document. Today, the Fourteenth Amendment touches almost every area of our daily lives, from politics to sex to religion to civil rights.

The Fourteenth Amendment requires states to observe the Bill of Rights. It bars the states from discriminating unfairly between races or sexes, or between locals and "outside agitators," or even between citizens and immigrants. It requires state elections to follow the rule of "one person, one vote."

If you feel free to criticize your mayor or governor, that's because the Fourteenth Amendment requires your state government to follow the First Amendment. (That's why Senator Pearce's constituents were free to campaign for his recall without fearing that he would use governmental power to punish them.) If you don't want your state government to outlaw your religious faith, or to funnel your tax funds to churches you don't support, that's because the Fourteenth Amendment applies the Religion Clauses against the states.

The amendment has been called "the second Constitution," because of the number and importance of the changes it made. But to hear many of the twenty-first century's far-right "constitutionalists" tell the American story, the Fourteenth Amendment doesn't exist. Or at least, not as something that affects the way we live today.

These people are what I call "Fourteenth Amendment deniers." Their radical right-wing agenda is much more attainable if the values of human equality, and basic civil and political rights, are read out of the document. So, like the bumbling Sergeant Schultz in the 1960s sitcom *Hogan's Heroes*, they look at the text and see "nothing—nothing!"

To understand the changes the Fourteenth Amendment made in the Constitution, we have to read its full text and analyze it in terms of the structure of the Union as it existed in 1866, when the amendment was framed.

First, the text. At more than four hundred words, the Fourteenth Amendment is the longest amendment ever added to the Constitution. It consists of five sections; each of them, in one way or another, puts limits on what the government of a state can do to its own people and to anyone—citizen or alien—who enters its border.

The first section is in many ways the most important today. In only eighty words, it makes four major changes to the ways states can carry on their business. First is the Citizenship Clause, which, as we've seen, extends American citizenship to virtually every native-born American. Before the Civil War, states controlled their own citizenship, and no one could be an American citizen who was not permitted to be a citizen of his or her state. The Constitution's text made no reference to race and citizenship, but the Supreme Court, dominated by pro-slavery justices, had in *Dred Scott* used "everybody knows" originalism to hold that no black American could ever be a citizen, since "everybody knew" that the framers didn't much care for black people.

Most Northerners and Unionists thought *Dred Scott* was wrong when it was decided; the Citizenship Clause wrote that verdict into the Constitution. Except for the children of diplomats, any child born in the United States is a citizen—regardless of who his or her parents may be. Any American citizen is now also a citizen of any state he or she chooses to live in, even if the people around those parts don't like their kind.

Like the *Dred Scott* Court, the Far Right is now using "everybody knows" originalism to torture the clause into something other than what it says. American citizenship, the text reads, is the birthright of "all persons born . . . in the United States and subject to the jurisdiction thereof." "Subject to the jurisdiction" is a commonsense provision: if people living in the United States can be sued by their American neighbors or arrested by local police, most lawyers would say, they are "subject to the jurisdiction" of the United States. Are undocumented aliens and their American-born children "subject to the jurisdiction"? On a trip to Arizona in 2011, I took a survey of the audience. How many believed that Justice of the Peace Lester Pearce, Russell's brother, would dismiss all criminal charges against the child of an undocumented alien, on the grounds that he or she was not "subject" to his jurisdiction?

Not a hand went up.

The Far Right, however, now claims that this is a Da Vinci Code provision. It really means "present legally as permanent residents." Thus, undocumented people aren't "subject to the jurisdiction," and their children—even children of foreigners legally here on tourist or student visas—aren't citizens.

There's one problem with this interpretation: it's bosh. The historical record, which anti-immigrant activists like Pearce misquote and distort, shows that the "subject to the jurisdiction" language applied in 1868 to only two groups: American Indians living on reservations and accredited foreign diplomats. Both groups in 1868 had special legal immunity. Neither could be sued in American courts or arrested by American sheriffs. They were not "subject" to U.S. jurisdiction. (Native people on reservations became citizens by law during the 1920s and no longer possess any special legal immunities.)

The legislative debates during the framing of the amendment are explicit about this; no one at either end of the spectrum questioned it until the 1980s. Even *The Making of America*, the mother document of Glenn Beck "constitutionalism," states in unqualified terms that the Citizenship Clause "gives every human being born or naturalized in the United States the RIGHT to citizenship. . . . The only exceptions are children born to foreign diplomats and children born to enemies during wartime occupation."[3] Then immigration became a useful political issue, and a new crop of "originalists" like Pearce suddenly "discovered" the Da Vinci Code meaning, which just happened to match their own political platform.

Let's look at the rest of Section 1. It has a definite theme: equality and inclusion in state affairs. The second clause states that American citizenship has certain "privileges or immunities" that states have no power to restrict. The two clauses that follow, interestingly enough, aim at equal rights not just for citizens but also for "persons"—that is, for everyone, alien or citizen alike. State governments must accord to every "person" both "due process of law" and "the equal protection of the laws."

Every American child is a citizen. States are to exclude none; to keep their hands off the rights of their citizens; to provide due process for all; to treat every human being equally. Move forward to Section 5—it says Congress, not state legislatures, has the power to enforce these guarantees.

The other three sections, which are mostly now obsolete, are worth reading as well, simply to note how aggressively each of them restricted state power: over voting rolls, over qualifications for office, and over state Confederate debts. The amendment as a whole is a radical reduction in the power of the states and a corresponding increase in federal authority. It's strong medicine. No wonder the Right wants to pretend it doesn't exist.

Over the 150 years since it was adopted, the federal courts have gradually accepted that Section 1 requires all states to live by the basic guarantees of the Bill of Rights. That means free speech, press, assembly, and petition; free exercise of religion; no established churches; fair criminal and civil procedures; and a list of basic unwritten rights that democracy requires government to observe.

The right resents the idea that the Bill of Rights binds state governments. They also hate the idea of human equality. Congressional authority over the states upsets them almost as much. So they have responded by claiming that the Fourteenth Amendment doesn't exist—or at least doesn't mean what it says.

The most radical of them simply proclaim that the Fourteenth Amendment wasn't validly adopted. Southern senators and representatives weren't seated in the Congress that proposed it at the end of the Civil War, they argue, so that body was illegitimate. In 1957, with the prospect of school desegregation staring it in its all-white face, the Georgia state legislature went so far as to pass a resolution declaring that "the so-called 14th and 15th Amendments to the Constitution of the United States are null and void and of no effect."[4]

This old white-supremacist myth lives on. Every now and then I meet someone who explains to me that the Fourteenth Amendment doesn't bind white males, who are "sovereign citizens," and only applies to a lower class of "Fourteenth Amendment citizens"—women, nonwhites, naturalized citizens, and aliens. One man in rural Oregon assured me that if a policeman stopped me for speeding, all I had to say was "I'm not subject to the Fourteenth Amendment" and the officer would be required to let me go. As a lawyer, I felt obliged to advise him not to try it.

More influential members on the current Far Right tersely admit the amendment is there, but insist it deals only with problems long in the past. It was only "intended" to deal with the freed slaves, they say; since there aren't any freed slaves today, we don't need to worry about it. Here's Glenn Beck running that scam: the Fourteenth Amendment was designed "to protect newly freed slaves and their children and guarantee their rights as citizens. Last I checked, I don't think we're having that problem anymore."[5] Senator Pearce, in his appearance on CNN, echoed that idea: the amendment "was written to give credit to the African Americans."

Pearce and Beck have drunk deep from the phony American history that right-wingers have begun to substitute for the real thing. David Barton, that indefatigable peddler of Christian-nation snake oil, breezily explains that "'the intent of Congress' [in enacting the Fourteenth Amendment] was clear: to make recently freed slaves citizens of the state in which they resided. Very simply—and very specifically—the Fourteenth Amendment was a badly needed racial civil rights amendment."[6]

When right-wing "originalists" use the words "simply" or "clearly," hold onto your wallet; they usually mean "deeply disguised in a way only I am allowed to explain." Even Barton grudgingly admits that "the wording of the Fourteenth Amendment, divorced from its purpose, seems to condone" a broader interpretation—even requiring states to observe the Bill of Rights at all times, "not just on racial civil rights issues." That's like Lester Pearce saying that "it would have been better" if the framers had used different words, but it doesn't matter because everybody knows they didn't mean what they said. The amendment can't mean what it *says*—that all persons are entitled to due process and equal protection, that all American children are citizens by birth, that states are bound not to abridge the "privileges and immunities" of American citizenship. That's "a totally revised and foreign interpretation," Barton says.[7]

It just can't mean that. He doesn't want it to mean that. It would be politically bad for the Right if it meant that. The voices in his head tell him it doesn't mean that.

Nothing in the amendment's text limits its protections to race; nothing in it says that "equal protection" doesn't cover discrimination by sex. Justice Antonin Scalia, no fan of women's rights, makes this problem disappear with "everybody knows" originalism. When the amendment was proposed, he said not long ago with his usual confident inaccuracy, "Nobody ever thought that that's what it meant."[8] (In historical matters, Scalia is not what we might call a detail man: in fact, a lot of people thought it did mean exactly that. Nineteenth-century feminists, male and female, were deeply involved in drafting and debating the amendment,[9] and many of them tried to use the Equal Protection Clause for feminist purposes almost at once, only to be rebuffed by male judges who sounded a lot like Scalia.)

If the Fourteenth Amendment means what it says, it also means that the Establishment and Free Exercise Clauses apply to state governments. Here's where the Bartons of the world get desperate: their project is for official state religions and government-imposed prayer and religious education, and, in their wildest dreams, maybe religious qualifications for voting and holding office. To fulfill that dream, they have to wish the Fourteenth Amendment away.

If the amendment means what it says, then states also have to live by the criminal and civil justice guarantees of the Bill of Rights—trial by jury, the right to counsel, and so forth. That part of the amendment rubs Rick Perry the wrong way. "[T]he Fourteenth Amendment," he writes, "is abused by the Court to carry out whatever policy choices it wants to make in the form of judicial activism."[10] A huge fan of the death penalty, Perry resents the very idea of federal rights interfering with the Texas injection gurney: "the states know best how they wish to punish criminals and for what crimes."[11]

The actual history is not disguised. The Fourteenth Amendment is a powerful, much-needed charter of civil and political rights for all, protecting much more than freedom from race discrimination.

Here's a voice Barton hasn't heard in his head—the voice of Senator Jacob Howard (R-MI), the Senate sponsor of the amendment, explaining that Section 1 incorporates

> the personal rights guaranteed and secured by the first eight amendments of the Constitution; such as the freedom of speech and of the press; the right of the people peaceably to assemble and petition the Government for a redress of grievances, a right appertaining to each and all the people; the right to keep and bear arms; the right to be exempted from the quartering of soldiers in a house without the consent of the owner; the right to be exempt from unreasonable searches and seizures, and from any search or seizure except by virtue of a warrant issued upon a formal oath or affidavit; the right of an accused person to be informed of the nature of the accusation against him, and his right to be tried by an impartial jury of the vicinage; and also the right to be secure against excessive bail and against cruel and unusual punishments. . . . The last two clauses of the first section of the amendment disable a state from depriving not merely a citizen of the United States, but any person, whoever he may be, of life, liberty, or property without due process of law, or from denying to him the equal protection of the laws of the state. This abolishes all class legislation and does away with the injustice of subjecting one caste of persons to a code not applicable to another.[12]

This is quite different—and far more radical—than Barton or Scalia's "original intent." The truth is that the Fourteenth Amendment changed the Constitution, and the country, in ways too numerous to count. That's not a mistake; that's not "judicial activism"; that's the Article V process at work, responding to history, to a brutal civil war, and to the will of the people. The Fourteenth Amendment's changes have made this a better country. Most particularly, it has made it one nation, where any citizen can live anywhere and believe and say anything he or she wants.

If you want to understand the alternative country the Right would like to create, listen to Rick Perry's explanation: "Federalism enables us to live united as a nation . . . while we live in states with like-minded people who share our values and beliefs. . . . If you don't support the death penalty and citizens packing a pistol, don't come to Texas. If you don't like medicinal marijuana or gay marriage, don't move to California."[13]

In Rick Perry's vision, the "like-minded people" of Texas can tell other Americans to shut up or get the frijoles out of town. That was the way things were run in much of the South before the Civil War. But in 1868, the American people decided that we'd all be better off if tin-pot local would-be dictators like Rick Perry or Russell Pearce had to answer to the higher authority of the Constitution.

It's important to note that actual federalism—the political competition and negotiation between state and federal governments, monitored by the voters—only works if the state governments play their proper role. The framers of the Fourteenth Amendment wanted to make sure that each state was democratically run, with fair elections, free speech, and an open political system that didn't tell minorities to go somewhere else. If state governments can ignore democratic values, their influence in national politics will be harmful; if they maintain open systems, they give the people a second voice in the handling of national problems.

The Perrys and the Pearces, though, still want back "their" America, a collection of local elite-run oligarchies where conformity is enforced by law. It's not a country most of us would want to live in.

We all have a stake in the Fourteenth Amendment. Attempts to mutilate it are aimed at the heart of contemporary American values. When a "constitutionalist" begins minimizing the amendment, it's a sign of ignorance—or something worse.

CHAPTER 9

Election of Senators Destroys "States' Rights"

Just after the 2010 election, Justice Antonin Scalia decided to explain the parts of the Constitution he doesn't like. "The Seventeenth Amendment has changed things enormously," Scalia said. "We changed that in a burst of progressivism in 1913, and you can trace the decline of so-called states' rights throughout the rest of the twentieth century."[1]

Scalia's comment nearly encapsulates the errors in one of the Far Right's most absurd crusades: to take the right of electing senators away from those idiots, the people, and give it back to the noble, disinterested members of the state legislatures.

Begin with the obsessive idea that life in America was pristine and joyous until a sudden "burst of progressivism," like an outbreak of measles, wreaked havoc with the political system. Add to that the idea that states have "rights" that should be protected against their own people. Conclude with the idea that the original design of the Senate was wise and noble, and that the squalor of today's Senate is due to our departure from the divinely inspired structure created in Philadelphia. All three ideas are flatly wrong.

Let's start with that "burst of progressivism." Here's Rick Perry's version of that myth: "the American people mistakenly empowered the federal government during a fit of populist rage in the early twentieth century by giving it an unlimited source of income (the Sixteenth Amendment) and by changing the way senators are elected (the Seventeenth Amendment)."[2]

In this version of history, the American people went out to celebrate New Year's Eve 1912, got drunk, and woke up with a tattoo.

The Seventeenth Amendment, which provides that senators from each state be "elected by the people thereof," was a key reform of the Progressive Era of American history. In recent years, the Far Right has come to the unlikely conclusion that American Progressives are in some way the shadow of Satan on Earth, responsible for every ill of contemporary American society. This requires believing two contradictory ideas at the same time. First, the changes they made were impulsive and almost accidental (the "tattoo" theory); second, they were also the result of a careful conspiracy to destroy liberty (the "sinister elite" theory). In Perryworld, Progressivism was both a mindless spasm by the ignorant masses *and* a carefully calculated conspiracy by the elite.

Perry writes that "the ethos of the Progressives" was "to exploit fear in order to exercise greater control rather than watching to see where the American imagination takes us." As for popular election of senators: "Oops. 'We the people' messed up. Or we were snookered."[3] (Perry says "oops" a lot.)

Glenn Beck sees Progressives as sinister totalitarians, not populists: "progressives believe that everyone innately *wanted* to do what was best for society, but, just in case they succumbed to greed or selfishness for a minute, there would be government 'supervision' in place to help them see the error of their ways."[4] In Beck's mind, Progressivism was imposed from above, by the evil triumvirate of Theodore Roosevelt, Woodrow Wilson, and Franklin D. Roosevelt. Just to take the craziness a little further, Andrew Napolitano of Fox News insists that the Seventeenth Amendment is actually unconstitutional, because it was added "at the height of the progressive era, when the government started telling us how to live."[5] (Remember the Tea Party leader who regards the Constitution as like the Bible, but only wants to count the first ten amendments.)

But whether Progressivism was the work of evil wizards or mindless dwarves, in the far-right fairy tale of American history, it sprang up overnight, like the magic thorns in Sleeping Beauty, strangling the Founders' republic and holding the American people in sinister thrall. We are waiting for a magic kiss to release the spell and return us to the good old days.

The foundation of the myth is that before the people messed it up with popular election, the Senate was a noble and disinterested institution, where gods in frock coats handed down wisdom to the hoi polloi. Here's former senator Zell Miller (D-GA): "Instead of senators who thoughtfully make up their own minds, as they did during the Senate's greatest era of

Clay, Webster and Calhoun, we now have many senators who are mere cat's paws for the special interests."[6] Conservative columnist George Will wrote in 2009 that "the Framers established election of senators by state legislators, under which system the nation got the Great Triumvirate—Henry Clay, Daniel Webster and John Calhoun—and thrived."[7]

This is a good example of how the Far Right distorts history. The problem is not merely their disdain for facts; the deeper problem is their insistence on seeing the past two and a half centuries as a fairy tale—noble princes, evil wizards, wicked spells—rather than as the complicated story of a nation finding its way by trial and error toward a more equitable and democratic system. To the Far Right, historical figures are either inerrant founts of divine wisdom—the Philadelphia framers, John C. Calhoun, Abraham Lincoln, Ronald Reagan—or subhuman plotters—Woodrow Wilson, Franklin Roosevelt, Earl Warren, Barack Obama. That's how story-book-land works; it's not how history operates. In order to understand the world we live in and the choices we face, we need to look at American history like adults blessed with memory and critical intelligence.

Let's start by speaking up for the maligned Progressive Era. It wasn't a spell of drunken popular madness; it also wasn't a sinister top-down conspiracy. In fact, it was an extraordinary thirty-year period of intense democratic excitement that occurred in direct reaction to the gross abuses of Gilded Age capitalism after the Civil War. The Gilded Age was much like today; the rich went on a rampage, gutting, by fair means or foul, any institution or principle that protected ordinary people against organized greed. At the end of it, the majority of the American people insisted, against enormous opposition, that the government's powers, structure, and values be modernized to reflect the interests of ordinary people rather than solely those of the wealthy.

Progressive reforms like the primary system; the initiative, referendum, and recall; the direct election of senators; suffrage for women; regulation of monopolies; and conservation of national parks and natural resources rose up from the serious, dignified demands of ordinary people, not from a top-down conspiracy or a sudden bout of madness.

After the Civil War, both federal and state governments had become the handmaidens of railroads, monopolies, and wealthy financiers. Protections for consumers and workers were virtually nonexistent. What Progressives wanted most was a system of government that protected ordinary citizens' economic interests against the growing power of concentrated wealth. Progressivism began to create a modern state apparatus that could regulate a modern economy. Progressivism went wrong in some areas— Prohibition, a Progressive cause, was, let's say, a mistake. But three other constitutional amendments during this period—the Sixteenth (progressive income tax), Seventeenth (election of senators), and Nineteenth (votes for women)—were triumphs of disciplined, popular mobilization against an arrogant, entrenched elite. It's hard to imagine our country functioning without any of the three.

The old noble Jedi senators are an even bigger, more damaging myth. Consider George Will and Zell Miller's "great triumvirate"—John C. Calhoun, Henry Clay, and Daniel Webster. Calhoun of South Carolina devoted his entire career to the care, feeding, and defense of human slavery, and to ensuring that the federal government would never interfere with that "peculiar institution." When he thought slave owners could control the federal government, he was for central power; when he realized they could not, he adopted "states' rights." Henry Clay of Kentucky worked to preserve the Union at the price of appeasing Calhoun and the South with virtually every protection for slavery they demanded. Even Daniel Webster, a Massachusetts man, threw in with slavery when the time came to defend the grotesque Fugitive Slave Act. Each man believed he was acting for the greater good, but they were wrong, and their blindness helped move the country toward destructive civil war.

And did the republic "thrive," as Will claimed? Well, yes, except for the slight detail of extending the slave system across the South and Southwest. And the other slight detail of a bloody civil war that led to nearly a million deaths. And, oh, yeah, the near-death experience of the American republic.

But otherwise it was just swell.

The Senate as firewall of slavery contributed strongly to the political paralysis that led to the Civil War. Much more greatness and the country would have been destroyed entirely.

When Reconstruction gave way to the Gilded Age, the Senate, still elected by the legislatures, became a different kind of firewall: the guardian of corporate privilege. It's that Senate that today's repeal advocates want back.

Remember what Zell Miller says: In the old days, senators made up their own minds; today they are cat's-paws for "the special interests."

It's a lie.

Hard as it may be to imagine, the Gilded Age Senate was in fact more subservient to established interests than the current one. It was during this period that the Senate came to be called "the Millionaire's Club," because industrial and banking magnates, having amassed huge fortunes, often bought themselves Senate seats so they could protect their wealth on the spot. It was easy to do: by 1890, the "special interests" *owned* the state legislatures. In 1906, journalist David Graham Phillips scored a publishing sensation with *The Treason of the Senate*, an exposé of corporate influence that gave rise to the term "muckraker." Phillips wrote that "the Senate is the eager, resourceful, indefatigable agent of interests as hostile to the American people as any invading army could be." That was because "a man cannot serve two masters. The Senators are not elected by the people. They are elected by 'the interests.'"[8]

Buying Senate seats, and senators, was a snap. It's a lot cheaper to bribe a small number of state lawmakers than to influence a statewide election. Railroads, banks, mining companies, and other corporations showered state officials with free passes, gifts, and outright bribes. In exchange, they dictated the names of the senators.

When special interests couldn't convince legislatures to back their stooges, they often simply refused to allow any senator to be named. Between 1890 and 1900, no fewer than fourteen Senate seats remained vacant because of legislative deadlock. In Oregon in 1897, the state government was so badly split over the Senate vacancy that the legislative session never happened at all—the state House of Representatives was unable to convene, and no senator was elected.

In some states, sergeants at arms tried to drag unwilling lawmakers into their capitols; in others, mobs tried to prevent legislative majorities from meeting. As George H. Haynes, the leading historian of the Senate, wrote in 1912, legislative elections of Senators had "led not merely to an occasional assault and to fist-fights of the mob, but to threats of organized attack and resistance, and to the reign of martial law."[9]

Popular opposition to the legislative election of senators was not a Progressive Era fad. Popular criticism of the system began only a few years after the Constitution went into effect. The first proposed constitutional amendment was introduced in 1826. But the movement finally became a serious political force in the 1880s. Over a thirty-year period, it became one of the most sustained and powerful popular mobilizations in American history.

When the Senate refused to approve the direct election amendment in 1910, popular fury led to the defeat—even under legislative election—of ten of the "no" votes at the next election. The new, purged Congress meekly agreed to the amendment; it was ratified by state legislatures in less than eleven months—one of the fastest ratifications in American history.

Finally, did the Seventeenth Amendment really in some way harm the states? Thomas Woods, author of *Nullification*, explains the harm this way: "Today, senators get elected by holding fundraisers in major U.S. cities and collecting donations from all over the country. This does not exactly make them beholden to their states."[10] The truth of that statement depends on what you mean by *state*. If by "California," say, you mean the people of California, Woods's statement is nonsense. When legislatures picked senators, out-of-state interests didn't seek influence by donations; they just selected the senators themselves and got them elected. This made the senators beholden to the interests, not "the state." Today, senators are still elected by state and are very aware that only the voters of their states can reelect them; anyone who visits Capitol Hill even for a short time will testify that they still work hard to represent their states' economic and social interests.

Senators also consult with governors and state governments and advocate for their interests on the floor. The state governments maintain effective lobbying presences in Washington, and, as a result, federal statutes often include language exempting state governments from their provisions. Many federal programs grant state governments a significant say in how federal programs are administered. (Even the much-maligned Patient Protection and Affordable Care Act prescribes a large role for the states, and the Obama administration has been ready to negotiate waivers of many of its requirements—as the statute permits—when state governments propose workable alternatives.) But the state's *legislators* don't call the shots: senators must closely attend to what their *voters* want if they want reelection.

As we've seen, the real objection to popular election is not that "special interests" have too much influence. They have less today than they did in the days of legislative election. Special interests spend freely to influence elections, but it's harder to tip a hundred thousand votes than to buy a hundred politicians.

The real objection appears when we ask what the words "special interests" really mean when used by the Right. In its original usage, "special interest" denoted private financial or business interests who sought to use government to increase their wealth at the expense of the public good. The term actually originated during the Progressive Era, as a description of the kind of organized wealth that dominated the federal government. That kind of "special interest" is certainly at work in Washington and around the country in the twenty-first century just as it was in the nineteenth.

But in the language of today's Right, banks, corporations, pharmaceutical companies, and oil giants are not "special interests"—they're "job creators," the heart of our economic system. When the Right uses the term "special interest," they are referring to groups that represent *the public*: consumers, industrial or agricultural workers, the poor, racial minorities, the disabled, the sick, and the hungry. These "interests"—the sinister interests of the broad public—are what the government must be defended against, if necessary by stripping the people of their right to elect public officials.

There's no question that broad-based national advocacy organizations have more chance to address their ideas to senators than they did in the days of legislative election. Senators must encounter and deal with people from all over the country, representing a variety of points of view, if they want to be effective in the capital and to advance in national politics. Endorsement or opposition from groups like the National Taxpayers Union, the National Rifle Association, the National Education Association, the Consumer Federation of America, and so on, can gain or cost them votes in their home states. Even in the post–*Citizens United* world, some broad-based reform groups can muster nearly as much influence at the polls as do the Koch Brothers.

This means that a popularly elected senator cannot be secure in office by consulting a few powerful business executives and political bosses back home; he or she must bear in mind the many diverse groups and interests in the electorate. This seems to reflect some of what James Madison himself defined as the purpose of representative government: "to refine and enlarge the public views, by passing them through the medium of a chosen body of citizens, whose wisdom may best discern the true interests of their country."[11]

Let's not be naive, however; we all know that, under current campaign finance law, senators don't just consult public interest groups. They accept multimillion-dollar contributions from corporate PACs and rich individuals to run their reelection campaigns. Would legislative election somehow change that? Well, yes—it would direct the flow of money from the senator's campaign committees directly to state legislators' bank accounts. And as I noted above, it would make buying a Senate seat a lot cheaper. If your idea of "states' rights" is "the right of local politicians to wet their beaks," then legislative election would be a great step forward.

Here's the nub of the argument: when the Far Right says the Seventeenth Amendment harmed "the states," they mean it harmed state legislatures. But state legislatures are not "the state"; they are simply another institutional player in our complex federal scheme. The "state," properly considered, is the people of the state. Even in a system dominated by big money, the voters still have a choice. Who is the better judge of the people's interests—the state legislature or the people themselves?

The Right's argument is that senators who are responsible to the voters rather than the local elite have taken away the states' "rights." What rights are they talking about? The Constitution nowhere mentions them. Properly viewed, in fact, governments and legislators do not have "rights."

A right is a prerogative that an individual can exercise exactly as he wishes. In America, you and I—ordinary citizens—have rights. When you exercise your right to free speech, you can say silly things, or smart ones, or you can just keep your mouth shut. If the Second Amendment guarantees a "right to bear arms," you can go out and buy a legal weapon, or you can decide not to bring guns into your home. You aren't accountable to anyone for the decision.

How can a state government have "rights" in this sense? Should state legislators have the "right" not to approve a budget because they don't feel like it? State governments, like the federal government, have *powers*. In the language of the Declaration of Independence, they "derive their just powers from the consent of the governed"—and they are required to exercise them, not to maximize their own power (or income), but to further the interests of the people.

Appropriate state powers are actually protected by the Constitution and by decisions of the Supreme Court. The federal government can offer incentives to state governments, but it cannot reach down and tell a state legislature what to do. Congress does not send representatives to vote in state legislatures; state governments should have no corresponding right to control Congress.

The silly campaign against the Seventeenth Amendment won't go anywhere; popular election is here to stay. But the Far Right's rhetoric on this issue is worth studying. It shows that much of the "constitutionalism" being peddled to the people is highly selective, and much of the history that supports it, like Will's fatuous yearning for the "Great Triumvirate," is pseudo-patriotic twaddle.

The real reason the Scalias, Millers, and Wills of this world favor repeal is simply this: a legislatively appointed Senate could be relied on to block progressive legislation. Believe it or not, they regard the current Senate—which gives an equal vote to tiny states and large ones, and which allows as few as forty senators to block any measure with a filibuster—as *too* democratic, *too* effective. The current Senate can't be counted on to block every progressive idea. Glenn Beck explains it this way: without popular election, "Obama's health care bill would never have seen the light of day."[12]

They want the Constitution to ensure their side never loses a vote.

To hell with that.

CHAPTER 10

International Law Is a Threat to the Constitution

Not long ago, Representative Sandy Adams (R-FL) introduced a bill to forbid the Supreme Court from ever citing or using any precedent from international law. In the conservative *Washington Times*, Adams explained:

> In recent years, Supreme Court justices have interjected international law into their rulings, creating an environment of disregard for national sovereignty and threatening the institutions put in place by our forefathers. The Constitution laid the foundation for our nation's judicial system, and allowing foreign law to supersede it in any capacity leads to its erosion. Not only is using international precedent a transparent disregard for the Constitution, but it could be used to advance a judge's personal political agenda over the best interests of the nation.[1]

Adams said she was outraged that the Court has discussed international law and human rights norms in three recent decisions: *Atkins v. Virginia*,[2] which held that executing the mentally retarded violates the Eighth Amendment; *Roper v. Simmons*,[3] which held that executing adults for crimes they committed as children does the same; and (most importantly) *Lawrence v. Texas*,[4] which held that jailing competent adults for consensual private sex with members of the same sex violates the Constitution's guarantee (in both the Fifth and the Fourteenth Amendments) of "due process of law."

It shouldn't surprise us that all three of these decisions expand individual rights under the Constitution and extend its protection to groups that people like Adams despise. Many conservatives loathe limitations on the death penalty; many also—let's not kid ourselves—loathe and fear gay men and lesbians. If courts are protecting the right to life of the retarded or of juveniles—if they are affording equality to gay people—foreigners must be to blame. Judges must be forced to stop their ears to this strange, seductive foreignness.

To the Far Right, international and foreign law is a legal bubonic plague, spreading out of control across our borders. The fear is inspired in part by opposition to human-rights norms and in part by religious and ethnic intolerance being systematically stirred up by conservative political figures for political gain.

Consider that in November 2010 the voters of Oklahoma amended their state constitution to state that judges in state courts "shall not look to the legal precepts of other nations or cultures. Specifically, the courts shall not consider international or Sharia Law."[5] Most voters probably focused on the "Sharia law" provision. In the years since 9/11, anti-Muslim hate groups have assiduously spread the fear that American Muslims are part of a secret conspiracy to place us all under the rule of the Quran and the mullahs. The Oklahoma initiative aimed to stigmatize and humiliate a small religious minority; that's shameful enough.

The sponsors of the initiative, however, had other purposes in mind as well. Their state constitutional amendment also purports to overturn Article VI § 2 of the United States Constitution. That section proclaims that "[t]his Constitution, and the laws of the united states which shall be made in pursuance thereof; and all treaties made, or which shall be made, under the authority of the united states, shall be the supreme law of the land; and the judges in every state shall be bound thereby, any thing in the Constitution or laws of any state to the contrary notwithstanding."

What does this have to do with the Oklahoma initiative? International law, or "the law of nations," comes from two sources: treaties and what is called "customary international law." After the amendment, then, Oklahoma's judges can't cite treaties in their decisions anymore. They may be the supreme law of the land, but not in Oklahoma.

There's little doubt that the measure passed because voters feared that somehow "Sharia law" would become binding American law, enforced against Christians and others by police and courts. Proponents invoked images of European blasphemy laws. Rogue judges, they implied, may decide that Oklahoma is part of the mythical worldwide Muslim "caliphate," or require Christian women to wear burkas in public. The fact that (as we'll see) this could never happen under the U.S. Constitution did not allay that fear; nor did the fact that Muslims constitute less than one-half of one percent of the population in Oklahoma.

Other Americans are afraid that they will awake one morning in a nation ruled by foreigners. *Red Dawn*, the 1984 movie starring Patrick Swayze in which Russian and Cuban troops take over Colorado, has such a deep hold on the American imagination that it has been remade in 2012 with North Koreans in the role of occupiers. (Some Americans really do fear that a nation of 24 million people, one of the poorest in the world, will take over a superpower of more than 300 million.) Recall that Lester Pearce, my instructor at "Constitution school," solemnly warned his students that criticism of Arizona for its anti-immigrant policies would inevitably lead to confrontations between blue-helmeted U.N. troops and pistol-wielding patriots on the streets of Phoenix.

Are we facing the specter of foreign troops enforcing strange laws? Do we need Patrick Swayze? What is the proper role of international law in the Constitution? For that matter, what is the "international law" that the Right professes to fear?

Much of the current criticism is actually aimed at U.S. courts' interpreting and applying *foreign* law, not international law. Foreign law involves the statutes of other countries and the decisions of national courts in those countries interpreting their own law. "International law" is somewhat different. It has two sources: binding treaties and "customary international law," which is derived by courts and legal authorities by studying the practices of countries and analyzing the norms they follow. Both treaties and customary international law are interpreted by courts in countries all over the world, and by international courts such as the European Court of Human Rights in Strasbourg, France, and the International Court of Justice (the "World Court") in The Hague, Netherlands.

What are the implications of using these sources of law in U.S. cases? Senators at the confirmation hearings for Justice Sonia Sotomayor asked her about her views on using foreign and international law. Her measured answer was instructive:

> American law does not permit the use of foreign law or international law to interpret the Constitution. . . . There is no debate on that question. There's no issue about that question.

> The question is a different one because there are situations
> in which American law tells you to look at international or
> foreign law. . . . So, for example, if the U.S. is a party to a
> treaty, and there's a question of what the treaty means, then
> courts routinely look at how other courts of parties who are
> signatories are interpreting that. There are some U.S. laws that
> say you have to look at foreign law to determine the issue. So,
> for example, if two parties have signed a contract in another
> country that's going to be done in that other country, then
> American law would say you may have to look at that foreign
> law to determine the contract issue.[6]

At her confirmation, Elena Kagan answered a similar question slightly differently. "There are some cases in which the citation of foreign law or international law might be appropriate," she said. As one example she cited *Hamdi v. Rumsfeld*,[7] the 2004 case interpreting whether the president could imprison a U.S. citizen without trial on the allegation that he was an "enemy combatant." Kagan said, "Justice O'Connor, in that case—one of the ways that she interpreted that statute was by asking about the law of war and what the law of war usually provides, what authorities the law of war provides. That's a circumstance in which, in order to interpret a statute giving the President various wartime powers, the court thought it appropriate to look to what the law of war generally provided."

Kagan noted that the Constitution gives the president the power to "receive ambassadors," and imagined a court challenge to a future president's decision to receive or reject a foreign representative's credentials: "There might be a question, well, who counts as an ambassador? One way to understand that question is to look at what international law says about who counts as an ambassador, and that might or might not be determinative, but it would be, you know, possibly something to think about and—and—and something to cite."[8]

Interestingly enough, these answers are not very different from the answer of Justice Antonin Scalia, who likes to play to the galleries with sweeping statements condemning foreign-law sources. At a debate with Justice Stephen Breyer at American University in 2005, Scalia said:

> I do not use foreign law in the interpretation of the United
> States Constitution. Now, I will use it in the interpretation of
> a treaty. In fact, in a recent case I dissented from the Court,

including most of my brethren who like to use foreign law, because this treaty had been interpreted a certain way by every foreign court of a country that was a signatory, and that way was reasonable, although not necessarily the interpretation I would have taken as an original matter. But I thought that the object of a treaty being to come up with a text that is the same for all the countries, we should defer to the views of other signatories, much as we defer to the views of agencies—that is to say if it's within [the] ball park, if it's a reasonable interpretation, though not necessarily the very best.[9]

So some foreign law is okay. In fact, some foreign law is mandatory. The same goes for international law, both treaty-based and customary. We can huff and puff about how much better the United States is than those other countries ("I doubt whether anybody would say, 'Yes, we want to be governed by the views of foreigners,'" Scalia said in the same debate, a few minutes after having admitted that sometimes we *must* be), but our country is part of an international legal order and has been since the day it was established. The question isn't whether we should apply international or foreign law, but when—and whether we are applying it correctly.

International law is part of the Constitution. Article I § 8 grants Congress the power "to define and punish . . . offenses against the law of nations," and "to declare war, grant letters of marque and reprisal, and make rules concerning captures on land and water." Article II empowers the president, with the advice and consent of the Senate, to "make treaties." Article III extends the judicial power of federal courts "to all cases, in law and equity, arising under this Constitution, the laws of the united states, and treaties made, or which shall be made, under their authority," and also "to all cases affecting ambassadors, other public ministers and consuls [and] to all cases of admiralty and maritime jurisdiction"; Article VI § 2, as noted above, says "treaties made or which shall be made under the authority of the United States" will form part of "the supreme law of the land . . . any thing in the constitution or laws of any state to the contrary notwithstanding."

All of these concepts—offenses against the law of nations, declarations of war, authorized privateering on the high seas, and most particularly treaties made by the United States—are at or near the core of what is called "international law." Their presence in the Constitution isn't an accident. The framers knew a great deal of international law, and what they knew, they liked. One of their fondest wishes for the Constitution was that it would produce a government with the will to observe America's international obligations, the power to make the states do the same, and the strength to require other nations to live up to theirs.

Introducing Madison's "Virginia plan" (which became the basis for the Constitution), Virginia governor Edmund Randolph explained to the Philadelphia convention that America needed a new constitution because the states were routinely violating the law of nations. Oliver Ellsworth, speaking in support of a plan to give judges a role in vetoing laws, noted that in domestic legislation "the law of nations also will frequently come into question. Of this the judges alone will have competent information."[10] One delegate proposed giving Congress the power to "define" offenses against "the law of nations" as well as "punish" them. James Wilson—later appointed by George Washington to the Supreme Court—opposed giving Congress power to "define" offenses: "To pretend to define the law of nations which depended on the authority of all the civilized nations of the world, would have a look of arrogance, that would make us ridiculous."[11]

In Federalist No. 3, John Jay warned that the recklessness of state governments might allow the United States to drift into war with Portugal, Spain, or Britain. "It is of high importance to the peace of America that she observe the laws of nations towards all these powers."[12]

In America's first major foreign-policy crisis, over neutrality in the war between France and Britain, President Washington warned that

> whosoever of the citizens of the United States shall render himself liable to punishment or forfeiture under the law of nations by committing, aiding or abetting hostilities against any of the said powers, or by carrying to any of them, those articles which are deemed contraband by the modern usage of nations, will not receive the protection of the United States against such punishment or forfeiture; and further that I have given instructions to those officers to whom it belongs, to cause prosecutions to be instituted against all persons, who shall, within the cognizance of the Courts of the United States, violate the law of nations with respect to the powers at war, or any of them.[13]

The examples could be multiplied almost indefinitely. The United States from its inception has been a force for international law. In major foreign-policy crises, our greatest presidents have tried to follow international law and to induce other nations to follow it as well. After both World Wars, the United States took the lead in trying to create a stable international legal order that would prevent war and permit peaceful trade. The United Nations, which arose out of the wartime alliance that defeated the Axis powers, was largely an American creation. The United States took a major role in the development of such major human-rights measures as the Universal Declaration of Human Rights and the United Nations Convention Against Torture and Other Cruel, Inhuman or Degrading Treatment or Punishment. Historically, from the time of the Founding, Americans have looked to the development of international law as a means of ensuring peace and developing democracy and human rights.

The fashionable revulsion against international law is of fairly recent vintage. It has nothing to do with "original intent" and everything to do with internal divisions. It is deeply wrong and dangerous.

As Sotomayor noted, courts not only *may* apply treaties and foreign legal concepts in proper cases, they also *must*. That goes, by the way, for the many international human-rights treaties to which the United States is a party—they may be part of "the supreme law of the land." Interpreting treaties may also mean paying attention to how courts in other treaty nations read them. Even if members of Congress think that may lead to some pretty dad-gum bad (read "liberal") decisions, the Constitution itself has made that choice, and neither Glenn Beck nor the voters of Oklahoma can repeal it.

What about the citation of foreign and international law in other constitutional cases? Let's look at the three decisions that so incensed Representative Adams. *Atkins* concerned a defendant with an IQ of 59. Does executing such a person violate the Eighth Amendment's prohibition on "cruel and unusual punishments"? In his majority opinion, Justice John Paul Stevens made a fairly straightforward investigation of the current laws of the American states and found that more and more of them had banned the practice. In a footnote, he noted the trend of opinion among mental health professionals about the capacity of defendants like Atkins to form "criminal intent." He surveyed polling data about public attitudes. This inquiry was entirely orthodox under existing precedent, which holds that the Eighth Amendment is to be interpreted by current standards of decency, not by a voices-in-the-head séance with the eighteenth century.

Stevens's "crime" (at least in Oklahoma) was that during his survey of nonlegal sources, he stated that "within the world community, the imposition of the death penalty for crimes committed by mentally retarded offenders is overwhelmingly disapproved." The citation was to an amicus brief duly filed with the Court by the European Union in an earlier case. "Although these factors are by no means dispositive, their consistency with the legislative evidence [from American states] lends further support to our conclusion that there is a consensus among those who have addressed the issue," he concluded.[14]

In other words, his offense was that, in considering whether a punishment is "cruel and unusual," he considered all available evidence that it is unusual, including a twenty-word mention of foreign practices. There's no indication that he permitted these foreign practices to *overrule* American law or change the meaning of the Eighth Amendment. As his opinion makes clear, foreign practice did not contradict an established American principle; it confirmed the emerging American rule. So minor was the role of the EU brief that not even Justice Scalia could be bothered to rail against it.

In *Roper v. Simmons*, the issue was the Eighth Amendment again. Can a state execute an individual for a crime he had committed while older than fifteen but younger than eighteen, the age of majority? The argument is that defendants this young are not fully capable of understanding the consequences of their actions. Fifteen years earlier, the Court had said yes. But in *Roper*, Justice Kennedy surveyed American practice again, and then included an extended discussion of the world consensus, looking both at treaties and other countries. When the earlier case was decided, he noticed, "Iran, Pakistan, Saudi Arabia, Yemen, Nigeria, the Democratic Republic of Congo, and China" allowed such executions. Since then, all had either abolished or disavowed it.[15]

Thus, Justice Kennedy wrote, "it is fair to say that the United States now stands alone in a world that has turned its face against the juvenile death penalty."[16] Justice Scalia dissented. His main point, as always, was that American courts should not consider whether a punishment is "unusual" today, but only if it was unusual in 1789, when the Eighth Amendment was adopted. He further said that "the basic premise of the Court's argument—that American law should conform to the laws of the rest of the world—ought to be rejected out of hand."[17]

If the majority in *Roper* had said that "American law should conform to the laws of the rest of the world," Scalia might have a point. But the real issue in *Roper* was what *American* law—the Constitution—requires. We know that the Eighth Amendment forbids "cruel and unusual punishments." The real dispute was over the meaning of the word "unusual." To Scalia, the word has a Da Vinci Code meaning: "unusual in the thirteen American states and England in 1789, as determined by me looking in the Big History Book." (Thus, branding, nose slitting, cutting off hands, and executing seven year olds, as well as flogging, might very well be permitted today, because somebody in 1787 thought they were okay.) To Justice Kennedy and the majority, the word means, as it has since about 1630, "not usual; uncommon; exceptional."[18]

That's not a new question in American law; our courts have been applying the Eighth Amendment that way for half a century. The more complex point is whether American courts should consider foreign practice in determining whether a punishment is "unusual." If America is the only country in the world permitting a certain form of punishment, can we really argue that the practice isn't unusual? The Eighth Amendment doesn't say "unusual only in the United States." Absent such a textual command, why would we want our courts to ignore facts about the world we live in?

Finally, consider the Court's opinion in *Lawrence v. Texas*. That case reversed one of the Court's most embarrassing recent decisions, *Bowers v. Hardwick*, which held, 5–4, that states could make it a crime for two adult men or two adult women to engage in private, consensual sex. In *Bowers*, the plurality breezily asserted that Western civilization uniformly condemned homosexuality. As Chief Justice Warren Burger wrote in his concurrence, "Decisions of individuals relating to homosexual conduct have been subject to state intervention throughout the history of Western civilization. Condemnation of those practices is firmly rooted in Judeao-Christian moral and ethical standards."[19]

So we begin with a conservative opinion invoking an international standard—that of "Western civilization" and "Judeo-Christian moral and ethical standards." Everyone in the West agrees with us, the plurality was saying; homosexuality is bad and can be outlawed. Surely if one side can invoke these standards, the other side must be permitted to show that the statement is, in fact, false. And that's what happened: in his opinion reversing *Bowers*, Justice Kennedy showed that this claim about deeply rooted, universal condemnation was not true *even at the time Burger was writing*. Kennedy then included two mild paragraphs noting that much of the "Judaeo-Christian" world had *also* turned away from legalized homophobia well before *Bowers* was decided. Among his evidence, he cited legal materials from the United Kingdom and the European Court of Human Rights.

In other words, the majority in *Bowers* had invoked an international consensus. Kennedy's use of foreign law in *Lawrence* had been designed to show that the previous Court had gotten that international consensus wrong. The *Lawrence* opinion didn't say that *Bowers* should be reversed because other countries didn't like it; the *Bowers* plurality had claimed the agreement of other countries. Kennedy wrote that that claim was false.

The objection to this citation, then, can't be that it looks outside the United States; instead, it must be that only one side can invoke international standards.

The three cases above aren't wrong because they cite foreign and international law—nor are they right because they cite it. It's perfectly possible to disagree with Kennedy's conclusions. But if the decisions are wrong, it can't be because they discuss foreign legal materials. That consideration, as we've seen, is inevitable. Our Constitution demands it.

Even Justice Scalia is willing to cite such materials in cases involving individual rights—if the materials support his position. "We must never forget that it is a Constitution for the United States of America that we are expounding," he thundered in dissent in a case called *Thompson v. Oklahoma*, a precursor to *Roper v. Simmons*. In *Thompson*, the Court narrowly held that defendants could not be executed for crimes they committed before they were sixteen. But having written that only American practice was relevant to that question, Scalia quickly added, "The practices of other nations, particularly other democracies, can be relevant to determining whether a practice uniform among our people is not merely a historical accident, but rather so 'implicit in the concept of ordered liberty' that it occupies a place not merely in our mores but, text permitting, in our Constitution as well."[20] That left the door open for future Scalia opinions citing international and foreign law to uphold claims that Scalia might find more congenial. The important point is not that it is foreign law, but that it agrees with him.

Should we worry about the use of foreign and international law? Yes and no. The question in each case is whether the Court has made careful, principled use of the sources it considers. Any opinion is subject to that criticism, and there's no question that judges should use such materials only in a principled way. But the real objection of the Far Right to decisions like *Atkins*, *Roper*, and *Lawrence* isn't really about the use of foreign law: it's about the interpretation of our Bill of Rights to protect groups—gays and lesbians, juvenile defendants, the retarded, foreign prisoners at Guantanamo—that they don't like. That argument ought to be carried out in the open.

Due process of law and equal protection *aren't* suspicious foreign concepts; they are American ideas. Over the past century, they have spread across the world—and citizens of many countries have reason to be grateful that *their* national courts didn't refuse to use these concepts because of their American origins. The reverse is also true: if we refuse to note what other countries are making of these ideas, we are turning our backs on our own heritage of law. We need a better understanding of them; we don't need protection from them, either by ethnocentric judges or by punitive legislators.

The Far Right suggests that the U.S. Constitution stands in some way apart from international law, immune from its norms and obligations. The notion is nonsensical. The very purpose of the Constitution was to *constitute* a country, a being on the international plane that could carry out its obligations and enforce its rights under international law. Delegates to Philadelphia knew that trying to get along without following the rules of the international game would quickly lead the United States into economic conflict, and eventually war.

The United States can't ignore other countries today any more than we could in 1787—less so, in fact, because as an economic and military power, we depend on the cooperation of other countries in matters of trade, diplomatic relations, war and peace, and human rights. Just as one example, the United States military carefully studies and applies international law because, in case of conflict, they want U.S. prisoners treated in accordance with its norms. As a law student, I had the good luck to study international law with a retired U.S. Navy admiral who had been the chief judge advocate of the Navy. He made it clear to us that the Navy, with ships on the seas all over the world, had a keen interest in knowing international legal norms and making sure that both the United States and foreign countries observed them. If international law could be ignored, then U.S. sailors would be in constant doubt about their safety on the high seas.

America's economic survival rests on a foundation of international law. Many lawmakers screaming loudest about the dangers of international law represent agricultural districts, where farmers depend for their livelihood on the validity of trade treaties and the ability to collect international debts. Many other screamers buy their Chinese-made goods at Wal-Mart—binding trade treaties make the prices there so delightfully low. Many American business executives become furious when other nations refuse to honor international trade norms opening their markets to U.S. goods.

The attack on international law is gathering force during a political cycle in which Republicans are attacking a Democratic president for not believing in something called "American exceptionalism." This term has been used by right-wing figures like Newt Gingrich and Rick Perry to demonize Barack Obama, to suggest that in some way he is not fully American. Gingrich likes to claim that Obama's ideas are really those of a "post-colonial Kenyan" or a "Saul Alinsky radical"; Mitt Romney says that Obama wants to make America into a European country. Why are they so insistent on this idea? Well, now that the phony claims about Obama's birth certificate have been exploded, the right-wing propaganda machine is spreading the same libel by different means. Obama, and progressives in general, are not "real" Americans—their intellectual forebears are African or European or even (why else would Gingrich keep saying "Saul Alinsky"?) Jewish.

It's an ugly form of coded racism and anti-Semitism, and it also makes hash of an important idea. The concept of "American exceptionalism," though not the term, dates back two hundred years. As historian Gordon Wood explains, "Our beliefs in liberty, equality, constitutionalism, and the well-being of ordinary people came out of the Revolutionary era. So too did our idea that we Americans are a special people with a special destiny to lead the world toward liberty and democracy."[21] American exceptionalism, since the dawn of our republic, has been used to argue that the American system need not be limited by the pessimistic, cynical assumptions of the Old World—that a free people needs neither kings nor dictators, that self-government does not have to degenerate into mob rule or Caesarism, that ordinary people are fit to rule themselves, and that people of different religions, races, and backgrounds can live together without an imperial state or an established church to keep them in their places.

Barack Obama is the son of a Kenyan immigrant and a single mother, raised in Hawaii, who has become the first African American president. The idea that such a person does not believe in this version of American exceptionalism is ridiculous. The Right keeps repeating it over and over because it's the only way to convince itself of something so absurd; even a second's thought exposes it as a crude lie.

Wood also explains that the original idea of American exceptionalism included a belief that the unique history of our country offered a chance to create a society "without both the corrupting luxury of Europe and its great distinctions of wealth and poverty."[22] The idea of economic equality is a good deal less congenial to the Far Right than is the idea of executing juveniles. "There is income inequality in America," Rick Santorum explained recently. "There always has been and, hopefully, and I do say that, there always will be."[23] In this view of America, the rich have every right to seize wealth and grind the faces of the poor, and the poor should thank them for it.

So they have reinvented the idea of "exceptionalism," turning it into what I call "American exemptionalism"—the idea that American society and government should be *exempt* from any legal or moral norm the powerful dislike. The nation they envision can invade other countries to enforce the U.N. Charter—but is exempt from that Charter's restrictions when they become inconvenient. It can lecture the world about human rights, but practice torture with impunity. It can demand respectful treatment of American citizens abroad, but refuse to recognize due process and treaty norms for treatment of foreigners—such as Mexican citizens facing the death penalty—at home.

The new version of "American exceptionalism," in other words, is just a high-sounding name for old-world thuggery. There's nothing about it that's either exceptional or American. Since the dawn of time, the strong have proclaimed that law does not apply to them. For centuries, our country's proudest "exceptional" moments have occurred on those occasions when we were willing to proclaim the reverse: that for all our power, our wealth, and our sense of our own special destiny, we were willing to live by norms that protect the weak and the poor as well as the strong and the rich. The current yammer about "American exceptionalism" is like the current claims of "constitutionalism"—both are systematic attempts to subvert and destroy the very concepts they claim to be exalting.

Thus, much of the attack on international law is fueled by hatred for any kind of law except the law of the jungle. Some of the rest of it stems from fear of imaginary dangers like "Sharia law." We have a First Amendment, which would easily deal with any attempt to govern Christians by Muslim precepts. That pesky Establishment Clause turns out to be very useful in such a case. The Oklahoma ballot initiative, for example, has been enjoined by the United States Court of Appeals for the Tenth Circuit. The court focused on the language specifically barring use of "Sharia law" in U.S. courts. The measure, it noted, doesn't bar the use of other religious law concepts in Oklahoma court proceedings. Instead, it singles out the religious heritage of Muslims for an official brand of invalidity. That violates the First Amendment's religion clauses by making Muslim people in Oklahoma unequal to everyone else.[24]

The decision to enjoin the initiative *doesn't* mean that the Mufti of Muskogee will now be free to convince dim-witted state judges to impose a burka rule on Christian women. That rule, too, would violate the Establishment Clause, which provides that the state can't enforce the norms of *any* religious tradition on dissenting citizens.

The opponents of "Sharia law" aren't content to rest on this bedrock guarantee. I suspect it's because—as we saw above—many of them are eager to gut the Establishment Clause. They want to impose Christian prayers and practices on the American people at large; indeed, some—think, for example, of Rick Santorum—have a larger ambition of bringing the entire nation under biblical law. They claim that American history gives government the power to endorse and enforce these Christian norms.

But without the Establishment Clause, is there any protection for *them* if they find themselves in a minority in the future? Like the character of William Roper in Robert Bolt's *A Man for All Seasons*, they want to "cut a great road through the law to go after the Devil." And like Roper, they have no answer when Bolt's Sir Thomas More asks, "And when the last law was down, and the Devil turned round on you—where would you hide, Roper, the laws all being flat?"[25]

A state that can require Christian Bible reading in public schools today might decide tomorrow that it wants the Quran, or L. Ron Hubbard's *Dianetics*, read in its place. A city that can post the Ten Commandments in courthouses today may want to post the Five Pillars of Islam tomorrow. Once the Establishment Clause is beaten flat, Christians may find themselves on the losing side. Only if the game is completely rigged—Christian okay, everything else forbidden—can they feel secure that their "Christian nation" will survive.

The real design of campaigns like Oklahoma's, then, is primarily to mobilize hatred against domestic out-groups and to brand political dissenters as infidels and traitors. To that extent, the outcry is dangerous. But far-right radicals also want to destroy America's heritage of fidelity to the rule of law. To the extent that they convince our courts to ignore what the Constitution requires, they will, in Wilson's words, make us ridiculous.

Afterword: The Battle Ahead

Of all the Founders, Thomas Jefferson retains a unique place in the American imagination. Tea Party types admire him so much that they invent quotations from him, but Bill Clinton, in the days before his first inauguration, also paid a ceremonial visit to Monticello to invoke Jefferson's spirit.

The reason, I suspect, is that—despite flaws and hypocrisies that no one who believes in real history would even think of denying—Jefferson remained, throughout his life, a confirmed optimist about America's future and its people. That spirit is shown in the words that form the epigraph of this book: "A little patience, and we shall see the reign of witches pass over, their spells dissolve, and the people, recovering their true sight, restore their government to its true principles."[1]

When those words were written, the political situation in the new nation—only twelve years after independence—was far darker than anything we face today. President John Adams's Federalist Party had outlawed criticism of the government or the president. Politically minded federal prosecutors were jailing newspaper editors, ordinary citizens, and even members of Congress who questioned Adams's policies. Congress had seriously considered a measure that would have allowed it to set aside the results of the coming presidential election. Even Jefferson, the sitting vice president, had to meet with friends and allies in secret lest he be accused of treason.

Yet Jefferson did not despair; indeed, he did not even question the bright future of the United States as a place where, in time, ordinary people would be able to order their own destinies, politically and economically, without a class of economic and social masters.

We need some of Jefferson's optimism today. Though the crisis is not as severe as 1798—yet—we do live, as Thomas Paine wrote in 1776, in "times that try men's souls."[2] Today as in 1798, concentrated wealth, tightly organized oligarchy, and unaccountable authority have their hands on the neck of our self-governing republic. One party does not even hide its complete devotion to the interests of the few; the other, also dependent on the rich, feebly resists the worst excesses of our new Gilded Age plutocracy.

Fear is abroad: economic uncertainty is morphing into fear of our own fellow citizens. Our problems, demagogues suggest, cannot lie in mere political errors; they must be the work of immigrants, Muslims, "secular humanists," and sinister progressives. Hard times always breed these phantom fears, but they do not arise out of nothing. As I write, one Republican presidential candidate has injected religion into the race by accusing Barack Obama of believing in "phony theology"; a second has accused him of being a "post-colonial Kenyan" and a "Saul Alinsky radical"; a third has claimed that instead of supporting American values, he represents "the worst of what Europe has become." Religion, race, nationality, and anti-Semitism are thus being consciously deployed for political ends. These are dangerous weapons, which in the end often turn on those who seek to harness them. Too often, as now, those who know better remain silent. Some hope to profit from the hatred and lies being sown abroad; others lack the words and the will to resist.

The toxic sludge overwhelming our national dialogue is now threatening to befoul one of our greatest national legacies—the oldest written constitution in the world, the heart of our republic.

As we've seen, the Constitution set in motion an elected government that has carried the United States through more than two centuries of struggle to the position of strength it occupies today. Having studied it for more than twenty years, I am well aware of its flaws, both past and present, but I am also aware that it has slowly, through historical lesson and amendment, slowly come to embody many American values we do not wish to give up or compromise: human equality, political freedom, the ability of free people to solve the problems of an uncertain present and an unpredictable future.

But the American Far Right has now targeted the Constitution for hostile takeover. Well funded, relentless, and unscrupulous, it has every reason to expect success. Consider that, in the past few decades, the reality of biological evolution by natural selection—established beyond rational doubt both by the fossil record and by laboratory research—has been transformed in the American mind into something faintly shady, a fanciful theory worthy at best of equal consideration beside fairy tales like "intelligent design" and creation by Thetans. The overwhelming scientific consensus that our planet is warming, and that human activity is the cause, has been met with such effective denial and disinformation that our system has been unable to fashion any response to this threat to human survival.

The Right today wants to do the same number on the Constitution. The text is there for all to read; the history is available to anyone with a library card. But these important truths are increasingly obscured by a cloud of David Barton–style lies, Da Vinci Code mysticism, and invented claims of "original intent."

Those who deploy these forces against our fundamental law are not "constitutionalists"; they are the witches of today. Their ideas do not come from the Founders they claim to revere, but from those who throughout American history have struggled to undo the Founders' work: the Anti-Federalists who opposed ratification of the Constitution; the Southern slave masters who split the country in two in 1861; the intellectual sycophants and legal hired guns of the Gilded Age robber barons; the racist ideologues who tried to block racial equality in the 1950s; the white separatists, militia thugs, and neo-Nazis who lurk today near places like Malta, Idaho.

That many of those on the right sincerely believe the bilge they are peddling is no excuse for the damage they are doing. Sincerity is often a virtue, but when coupled with political narcissism, laziness, and hatred, it is a dangerous, addictive vice. The snake oil salesman may believe that his elixir really cures all ills, but that belief does not help those who buy it and get sick.

Throughout history, fools have probably done more damage than have knaves.

Make no mistake: the aim of the "constitutionalists" of today is not liberty of a kind we would recognize. "Liberty to steal the didies off of babies!" Sinclair Lewis wrote in 1935. "I tell you, an honest man gets sick when he hears the word 'Liberty' today, after what the Republicans did to it!"[3] The liberty the Right offers is at best the liberty to survive in the cracks of a crumbling economy, the liberty to send your children to collapsing schools, the liberty to go bankrupt when major illness strikes, and the liberty to approach old age with dread because Wall Street pirates have made off with your pension. It is the liberty to seek help that will not come from a government that does not care.

It is the liberty to live in a declining society, to watch the United States tumble from first-world to third-world status in one generation.

Real liberty—political freedom, self-government, and individual rights—is not on the right-wing agenda.

So the stakes are high. But the battle can be won. It has been fought, and won, before in American history. The reason the Far Right hates the Progressive Era so deeply is that it represents the latest victory in the on-going struggle over what sort of country we will live in. During the last part of the nineteenth and the early twentieth centuries, ordinary people demanded reform and modernization from their government. The forces of Gilded Age capitalism were as daunting and ruthless as those we face today; their intellectual hirelings were as arrogant and sarcastic as Glenn Beck and Andrew Napolitano, but they lost the battle nonetheless. Just so, today, armed with common sense, the Constitution, and a touch of Jefferson's optimism, we can keep our republic.

Constitutional struggles seem to take place over our heads—in the Supreme Court, in Congress, and in elite institutions that employ legions of brilliant lawyers to fight for their interests. It is easy to feel hopeless and outgunned. But the battle is to be won or lost as much in the minds of ordinary Americans as in law schools or courtrooms. If we are prepared to resist the nonsense being preached about the Constitution, we have the tools to do so.

What can an ordinary American do?

Arm yourself with knowledge. The truth about the Constitution and its place in history are available to anyone. This book is far from the final word; every citizen owes it to him- or herself to forge an individual under-standing of the Constitution. There is a reading list at the end of this book that will provide an excellent starting point for anyone who wants a deeper understanding of the Constitution. The books suggested are not written primarily for lawyers or specialists; they can be understood and enjoyed by anyone with a little patience and an interest in American government and history. As you learn more, your nose for nonsense will grow keener.

Join with your neighbors. As we have seen during the past four years, movements like the Tea Party spring out of groups of like-minded people who meet together and plan political action. Progressive citizen groups can play a powerful role in mobilizing public opinion and challenging lies and distortions in the national dialogue. You may already belong to a group that meets to discuss national politics, books, or ideas generally. If you do, suggest that your group study the Constitution. Read a book like Akhil Amar's *America's Constitution: A Biography* or Richard Beeman's *Plain, Honest Men* as a group project. Find speakers with genuine credentials in law, history, or government to address your group on the Constitution's meaning and its history. Arguing about the Constitution is, as much as baseball, America's national pastime. The more you do it, the more you'll enjoy it—and the less you will feel intimidated and silenced by right-wing con men and bullies in your community. And when you bring constitutional issues into politics, politicians will be obliged to respond.

Speak up. The current crop of lies takes root in the silence of those who know better, or who should. No matter where you live—major city, small town, or rural community—your local media are filled with discussions of political and constitutional issues. The Far Right makes use of letters, columns, and political town meetings to spread its ideas; those who know better must be willing to answer them when they do. Often people ask me whether it is worth tangling with the Far Right on these issues: after all, we will never convince Tea Partiers that the Fourteenth Amendment really exists, or that the Progressive Era was not an alien conspiracy, or that factory owners don't have a divine right to exploit children. That's true, but it misses the point. The audience we need to reach is not those on the other side whose minds are made up; it is those whose voices are not heard, who haven't made up their minds, who genuinely don't know whether the nonsense they are hearing is true or not.

"Reason by degrees submits to absurdity as the eye is in time accommodated to darkness," Samuel Johnson wrote 250 years ago.[4] Absurdity has gone unchallenged too long. So join the battle. If the local editorial columnist, or your congressman, or a self-styled patriot, publicly spreads nonsense about the Constitution, call them out. Write your own letter to the editor; call the congressman's office; challenge the blowhard to a debate. If you aren't ready to debate yourself, find someone who will. Don't sit idly by while lies take on the sheen of truth.

Monitor your community. The Far Right has targeted local schools and governments as recruiting grounds for its crusade. The National Center for Constitutional Studies asks local school boards to adopt its racist, flat-earth materials as official textbooks for high school government classes. This is as gross a violation of the Constitution—to say nothing of educational ethics—as it would be to designate the Quran as a history textbook. NCCS officials have also convinced some town governments to sponsor official programs teaching their nonsense to the community. Concern yourself with what is being taught to children and adults in your town. Make sure that presentations are based in text and history. It's not enough that far-right materials are "answered" by "equal time" for the truth. Falsehoods aren't entitled to equality with facts.

Find allies. It's easy to feel isolated and a little crazy when you set out to oppose the current right-wing constitutional jihad. But there are lawyers, scholars, and groups across the country who are as concerned as you are with what is being said and taught in the name of the Constitution. Find them—local attorneys who have genuinely studied the Constitution and might welcome a chance to speak about it; professors at nearby colleges and law schools who have a real claim to knowledge and understanding of the Constitution; advocacy groups in the states and in Washington, D.C., that stand ready to send materials and speakers to community groups who want to spread the word.

A year ago, when I published the first essay that eventually turned into this book, I made an offer that a number of groups—ranging from Portland, Oregon, to Phoenix, Arizona, to Newark, New Jersey—have taken me up on. Here it is again: If you have a group, large or small, that wants to understand the Constitution and the threats to it, get in touch with me. If I can, I will come to speak to your group; if I can't, I will try to help you find someone who can.

You're not alone. In fact, we are the majority. We have the resources to repel this assault on our deepest values by a small, determined minority. The only question is whether we have the will.

The Far Right likes to say, "We want our country back." Well, it's not their country; it belongs to all of us. And it's not their Constitution. If we stand by and let them wreck it, then shame on us.

The Constitution of the United States of America*

We the People of the United States, in Order to form a more perfect Union, establish Justice, insure domestic Tranquility, provide for the common defence, promote the general Welfare, and secure the Blessings of Liberty to ourselves and our Posterity, do ordain and establish this Constitution for the United States of America.

Article. I.

SECTION. 1.

All legislative Powers herein granted shall be vested in a Congress of the United States, which shall consist of a Senate and House of Representatives.

SECTION. 2.

The House of Representatives shall be composed of Members chosen every second Year by the People of the several States, and the Electors in each State shall have the Qualifications requisite for Electors of the most numerous Branch of the State Legislature.

---

* *Source*: National Archives, "The Charters of Freedom: 'A New World is at Hand,'" www
.archives.gov/exhibits/charters.

No Person shall be a Representative who shall not have attained to the Age of twenty five Years, and been seven Years a Citizen of the United States, and who shall not, when elected, be an Inhabitant of that State in which he shall be chosen.

Representatives and direct Taxes shall be apportioned among the several States which may be included within this Union, according to their respective Numbers, which shall be determined by adding to the whole Number of free Persons, including those bound to Service for a Term of Years, and excluding Indians not taxed, three fifths of all other Persons. The actual Enumeration shall be made within three Years after the first Meeting of the Congress of the United States, and within every subsequent Term of ten Years, in such Manner as they shall by Law direct. The Number of Representatives shall not exceed one for every thirty Thousand, but each State shall have at Least one Representative; and until such enumeration shall be made, the State of New Hampshire shall be entitled to chuse three, Massachusetts eight, Rhode-Island and Providence Plantations one, Connecticut five, New-York six, New Jersey four, Pennsylvania eight, Delaware one, Maryland six, Virginia ten, North Carolina five, South Carolina five, and Georgia three.

When vacancies happen in the Representation from any State, the Executive Authority thereof shall issue Writs of Election to fill such Vacancies.

The House of Representatives shall chuse their Speaker and other Officers; and shall have the sole Power of Impeachment.

SECTION. 3.

The Senate of the United States shall be composed of two Senators from each State, chosen by the Legislature thereof for six Years; and each Senator shall have one Vote.

Immediately after they shall be assembled in Consequence of the first Election, they shall be divided as equally as may be into three Classes. The Seats of the Senators of the first Class shall be vacated at the Expiration of the second Year, of the second Class at the Expiration of the fourth Year, and of the third Class at the Expiration of the sixth Year, so that one third may be chosen every second Year; and if Vacancies happen by Resignation, or otherwise, during the Recess of the Legislature of any State, the Executive thereof may make temporary Appointments until the next Meeting of the Legislature, which shall then fill such Vacancies.

No Person shall be a Senator who shall not have attained to the Age of thirty Years, and been nine Years a Citizen of the United States, and who shall not, when elected, be an Inhabitant of that State for which he shall be chosen.

The Vice President of the United States shall be President of the Senate, but shall have no Vote, unless they be equally divided.

The Senate shall chuse their other Officers, and also a President pro tempore, in the Absence of the Vice President, or when he shall exercise the Office of President of the United States.

The Senate shall have the sole Power to try all Impeachments. When sitting for that Purpose, they shall be on Oath or Affirmation. When the President of the United States is tried, the Chief Justice shall preside: And no Person shall be convicted without the Concurrence of two thirds of the Members present.

Judgment in Cases of Impeachment shall not extend further than to removal from Office, and disqualification to hold and enjoy any Office of honor, Trust or Profit under the United States: but the Party convicted shall nevertheless be liable and subject to Indictment, Trial, Judgment and Punishment, according to Law.

SECTION. 4.

The Times, Places and Manner of holding Elections for Senators and Representatives, shall be prescribed in each State by the Legislature thereof; but the Congress may at any time by Law make or alter such Regulations, except as to the Places of chusing Senators.

The Congress shall assemble at least once in every Year, and such Meeting shall be on the first Monday in December, unless they shall by Law appoint a different Day.

SECTION. 5.

Each House shall be the Judge of the Elections, Returns and Qualifications of its own Members, and a Majority of each shall constitute a Quorum to do Business; but a smaller Number may adjourn from day to day, and may be authorized to compel the Attendance of absent Members, in such Manner, and under such Penalties as each House may provide.

Each House may determine the Rules of its Proceedings, punish its Members for disorderly Behaviour, and, with the Concurrence of two thirds, expel a Member.

Each House shall keep a Journal of its Proceedings, and from time to time publish the same, excepting such Parts as may in their Judgment require Secrecy; and the Yeas and Nays of the Members of either House on any question shall, at the Desire of one fifth of those Present, be entered on the Journal.

Neither House, during the Session of Congress, shall, without the Consent of the other, adjourn for more than three days, nor to any other Place than that in which the two Houses shall be sitting.

SECTION. 6.

The Senators and Representatives shall receive a Compensation for their Services, to be ascertained by Law, and paid out of the Treasury of the United States. They shall in all Cases, except Treason, Felony and Breach of the Peace, be privileged from Arrest during their Attendance at the Session of their respective Houses, and in going to and returning from the same; and for any Speech or Debate in either House, they shall not be questioned in any other Place.

No Senator or Representative shall, during the Time for which he was elected, be appointed to any civil Office under the Authority of the United States, which shall have been created, or the Emoluments whereof shall have been encreased during such time; and no Person holding any Office under the United States, shall be a Member of either House during his Continuance in Office.

SECTION. 7.

All Bills for raising Revenue shall originate in the House of Representatives; but the Senate may propose or concur with Amendments as on other Bills.

Every Bill which shall have passed the House of Representatives and the Senate, shall, before it become a Law, be presented to the President of the United States: If he approve he shall sign it, but if not he shall return it, with his Objections to that House in which it shall have originated, who shall enter the Objections at large on their Journal, and proceed to reconsider it. If after such Reconsideration two thirds of that House shall agree to pass the Bill, it shall be sent, together with the Objections, to the other House, by which it shall likewise be reconsidered, and if approved by two thirds of that House, it shall become a Law. But in all such Cases the Votes of both Houses shall be determined by yeas and Nays, and the Names of the Persons voting for and against the Bill shall be entered on the Journal of each House respectively. If any Bill shall not be returned by the President within ten Days (Sundays excepted) after it shall have been presented to him, the Same shall be a Law, in like Manner as if he had signed it, unless the Congress by their Adjournment prevent its Return, in which Case it shall not be a Law.

Every Order, Resolution, or Vote to which the Concurrence of the Senate and House of Representatives may be necessary (except on a question of Adjournment) shall be presented to the President of the United States; and before the Same shall take Effect, shall be approved by him, or being disapproved by him, shall be repassed by two thirds of the Senate and House of Representatives, according to the Rules and Limitations prescribed in the Case of a Bill.

SECTION. 8.

The Congress shall have Power To lay and collect Taxes, Duties, Imposts and Excises, to pay the Debts and provide for the common Defence and general Welfare of the United States; but all Duties, Imposts and Excises shall be uniform throughout the United States;

To borrow Money on the credit of the United States;

To regulate Commerce with foreign Nations, and among the several States, and with the Indian Tribes;

To establish an uniform Rule of Naturalization, and uniform Laws on the subject of Bankruptcies throughout the United States;

To coin Money, regulate the Value thereof, and of foreign Coin, and fix the Standard of Weights and Measures;

To provide for the Punishment of counterfeiting the Securities and current Coin of the United States;

To establish Post Offices and post Roads;

To promote the Progress of Science and useful Arts, by securing for limited Times to Authors and Inventors the exclusive Right to their respective Writings and Discoveries;

To constitute Tribunals inferior to the supreme Court;

To define and punish Piracies and Felonies committed on the high Seas, and Offences against the Law of Nations;

To declare War, grant Letters of Marque and Reprisal, and make Rules concerning Captures on Land and Water;

To raise and support Armies, but no Appropriation of Money to that Use shall be for a longer Term than two Years;

To provide and maintain a Navy;

To make Rules for the Government and Regulation of the land and naval Forces;

To provide for calling forth the Militia to execute the Laws of the Union, suppress Insurrections and repel Invasions;

To provide for organizing, arming, and disciplining, the Militia, and for governing such Part of them as may be employed in the Service of the United States, reserving to the States respectively, the Appointment of the Officers, and the Authority of training the Militia according to the discipline prescribed by Congress;

To exercise exclusive Legislation in all Cases whatsoever, over such District (not exceeding ten Miles square) as may, by Cession of particular States, and the Acceptance of Congress, become the Seat of the Government of the United States, and to exercise like Authority over all Places purchased by the Consent of the Legislature of the State in which the Same shall be, for the Erection of Forts, Magazines, Arsenals, dock-Yards, and other needful Buildings;—And

To make all Laws which shall be necessary and proper for carrying into Execution the foregoing Powers, and all other Powers vested by this Constitution in the Government of the United States, or in any Department or Officer thereof.

SECTION. 9.

The Migration or Importation of such Persons as any of the States now existing shall think proper to admit, shall not be prohibited by the Congress prior to the Year one thousand eight hundred and eight, but a Tax or duty may be imposed on such Importation, not exceeding ten dollars for each Person.

The Privilege of the Writ of Habeas Corpus shall not be suspended, unless when in Cases of Rebellion or Invasion the public Safety may require it.

No Bill of Attainder or ex post facto Law shall be passed.

No Capitation, or other direct, Tax shall be laid, unless in Proportion to the Census or enumeration herein before directed to be taken.

No Tax or Duty shall be laid on Articles exported from any State.

No Preference shall be given by any Regulation of Commerce or Revenue to the Ports of one State over those of another; nor shall Vessels bound to, or from, one State, be obliged to enter, clear, or pay Duties in another.

No Money shall be drawn from the Treasury, but in Consequence of Appropriations made by Law; and a regular Statement and Account of the Receipts and Expenditures of all public Money shall be published from time to time.

No Title of Nobility shall be granted by the United States: And no Person holding any Office of Profit or Trust under them, shall, without the Consent of the Congress, accept of any present, Emolument, Office, or Title, of any kind whatever, from any King, Prince, or foreign State.

SECTION. 10.

No State shall enter into any Treaty, Alliance, or Confederation; grant Letters of Marque and Reprisal; coin Money; emit Bills of Credit; make any Thing but gold and silver Coin a Tender in Payment of Debts; pass any Bill of Attainder, ex post facto Law, or Law impairing the Obligation of Contracts, or grant any Title of Nobility.

No State shall, without the Consent of the Congress, lay any Imposts or Duties on Imports or Exports, except what may be absolutely necessary for executing it's inspection Laws: and the net Produce of all Duties and Imposts, laid by any State on Imports or Exports, shall be for the Use of the Treasury of the United States; and all such Laws shall be subject to the Revision and Controul of the Congress.

No State shall, without the Consent of Congress, lay any Duty of Tonnage, keep Troops, or Ships of War in time of Peace, enter into any Agreement or Compact with another State, or with a foreign Power, or engage in War, unless actually invaded, or in such imminent Danger as will not admit of delay.

Article. II.

SECTION. 1.

The executive Power shall be vested in a President of the United States of America. He shall hold his Office during the Term of four Years, and, together with the Vice President, chosen for the same Term, be elected, as follows:

Each State shall appoint, in such Manner as the Legislature thereof may direct, a Number of Electors, equal to the whole Number of Senators and Representatives to which the State may be entitled in the Congress: but no Senator or Representative, or Person holding an Office of Trust or Profit under the United States, shall be appointed an Elector.

The Electors shall meet in their respective States, and vote by Ballot for two Persons, of whom one at least shall not be an Inhabitant of the same State with themselves. And they shall make a List of all the Persons voted for, and of the Number of Votes for each; which List they shall sign and certify, and transmit sealed to the Seat of the Government of the United States, directed to the President of the Senate. The President of the Senate shall, in the Presence of the Senate and House of Representatives, open all the Certificates, and the Votes shall then be counted. The Person having the greatest Number of Votes shall be the President, if such Number be a Majority of the whole Number of Electors appointed; and if there be more than one who have such Majority, and have an equal Number of Votes, then the House of Representatives shall immediately chuse by Ballot one of them for President; and if no Person have a Majority, then from the five highest on the List the said House shall in like Manner chuse the President. But in chusing the President, the Votes shall be taken by States, the Representation from each State having one Vote; A quorum for this purpose shall consist of a Member or Members from two thirds of the States, and a Majority of all the States shall be necessary to a Choice. In every Case, after the Choice of the President, the Person having the greatest Number of Votes of the Electors shall be the Vice President. But if there should remain two or more who have equal Votes, the Senate shall chuse from them by Ballot the Vice President.

The Congress may determine the Time of chusing the Electors, and the Day on which they shall give their Votes; which Day shall be the same throughout the United States.

No Person except a natural born Citizen, or a Citizen of the United States, at the time of the Adoption of this Constitution, shall be eligible to the Office of President; neither shall any Person be eligible to that Office who shall not have attained to the Age of thirty five Years, and been fourteen Years a Resident within the United States.

In Case of the Removal of the President from Office, or of his Death, Resignation, or Inability to discharge the Powers and Duties of the said Office, the Same shall devolve on the Vice President, and the Congress may by Law provide for the Case of Removal, Death, Resignation or Inability, both of the President and Vice President, declaring what Officer shall then act as President, and such Officer shall act accordingly, until the Disability be removed, or a President shall be elected.

The President shall, at stated Times, receive for his Services, a Compensation, which shall neither be increased nor diminished during the Period for which he shall have been elected, and he shall not receive within that Period any other Emolument from the United States, or any of them.

Before he enter on the Execution of his Office, he shall take the following Oath or Affirmation:—"I do solemnly swear (or affirm) that I will faithfully execute the Office of President of the United States, and will to the best of my Ability, preserve, protect and defend the Constitution of the United States."

SECTION. 2.

The President shall be Commander in Chief of the Army and Navy of the United States, and of the Militia of the several States, when called into the actual Service of the United States; he may require the Opinion, in writing, of the principal Officer in each of the executive Departments, upon any Subject relating to the Duties of their respective Offices, and he shall have Power to grant Reprieves and Pardons for Offences against the United States, except in Cases of Impeachment.

He shall have Power, by and with the Advice and Consent of the Senate, to make Treaties, provided two thirds of the Senators present concur; and he shall nominate, and by and with the Advice and Consent of the Senate, shall appoint Ambassadors, other public Ministers and Consuls, Judges of the supreme Court, and all other Officers of the United States, whose Appointments are not herein otherwise provided for, and which shall be established by Law: but the Congress may by Law vest the Appointment of such inferior Officers, as they think proper, in the President alone, in the Courts of Law, or in the Heads of Departments.

The President shall have Power to fill up all Vacancies that may happen during the Recess of the Senate, by granting Commissions which shall expire at the End of their next Session.

SECTION. 3.

He shall from time to time give to the Congress Information of the State of the Union, and recommend to their Consideration such Measures as he shall judge necessary and expedient; he may, on extraordinary Occasions, convene both Houses, or either of them, and in Case of Disagreement between them, with Respect to the Time of Adjournment, he may adjourn them to such Time as he shall think proper; he shall receive Ambassadors and other public Ministers; he shall take Care that the Laws be faithfully executed, and shall Commission all the Officers of the United States.

SECTION. 4.

The President, Vice President and all civil Officers of the United States, shall be removed from Office on Impeachment for, and Conviction of, Treason, Bribery, or other high Crimes and Misdemeanors.

Article III.

SECTION. 1.

The judicial Power of the United States shall be vested in one supreme Court, and in such inferior Courts as the Congress may from time to time ordain and establish. The Judges, both of the supreme and inferior Courts, shall hold their Offices during good Behaviour, and shall, at stated Times, receive for their Services a Compensation, which shall not be diminished during their Continuance in Office.

SECTION. 2.

The judicial Power shall extend to all Cases, in Law and Equity, arising under this Constitution, the Laws of the United States, and Treaties made, or which shall be made, under their Authority;—to all Cases affecting Ambassadors, other public Ministers and Consuls;—to all Cases of admiralty and maritime Jurisdiction;—to Controversies to which the United States shall be a Party;—to Controversies between two or more States;—between a State and Citizens of another State,—between Citizens of different States,—between Citizens of the same State claiming Lands under Grants of different States, and between a State, or the Citizens thereof, and for-eign States, Citizens or Subjects.

In all Cases affecting Ambassadors, other public Ministers and Consuls, and those in which a State shall be Party, the supreme Court shall have original Jurisdiction. In all the other Cases before mentioned, the supreme Court shall have appellate Jurisdiction, both as to Law and Fact, with such Exceptions, and under such Regulations as the Congress shall make.

The Trial of all Crimes, except in Cases of Impeachment, shall be by Jury; and such Trial shall be held in the State where the said Crimes shall have been committed; but when not committed within any State, the Trial shall be at such Place or Places as the Congress may by Law have directed.

SECTION. 3.

Treason against the United States, shall consist only in levying War against them, or in adhering to their Enemies, giving them Aid and Comfort. No Person shall be convicted of Treason unless on the Testimony of two Witnesses to the same overt Act, or on Confession in open Court.

The Congress shall have Power to declare the Punishment of Treason, but no Attainder of Treason shall work Corruption of Blood, or Forfeiture except during the Life of the Person attainted.

Article. IV.

SECTION. 1.

Full Faith and Credit shall be given in each State to the public Acts, Records, and judicial Proceedings of every other State. And the Congress may by general Laws prescribe the Manner in which such Acts, Records and Proceedings shall be proved, and the Effect thereof.

SECTION. 2.

The Citizens of each State shall be entitled to all Privileges and Immunities of Citizens in the several States.

A Person charged in any State with Treason, Felony, or other Crime, who shall flee from Justice, and be found in another State, shall on Demand of the executive Authority of the State from which he fled, be delivered up, to be removed to the State having Jurisdiction of the Crime.

No Person held to Service or Labour in one State, under the Laws thereof, escaping into another, shall, in Consequence of any Law or Regulation therein, be discharged from such Service or Labour, but shall be delivered up on Claim of the Party to whom such Service or Labour may be due.

SECTION. 3.

New States may be admitted by the Congress into this Union; but no new State shall be formed or erected within the Jurisdiction of any other State; nor any State be formed by the Junction of two or more States, or Parts of States, without the Consent of the Legislatures of the States concerned as well as of the Congress.

The Congress shall have Power to dispose of and make all needful Rules and Regulations respecting the Territory or other Property belonging to the United States; and nothing in this Constitution shall be so construed as to Prejudice any Claims of the United States, or of any particular State.

SECTION. 4.

The United States shall guarantee to every State in this Union a Republican Form of Government, and shall protect each of them against Invasion; and on Application of the Legislature, or of the Executive (when the Legislature cannot be convened), against domestic Violence.

Article. V.

The Congress, whenever two thirds of both Houses shall deem it necessary, shall propose Amendments to this Constitution, or, on the Application of the Legislatures of two thirds of the several States, shall call a Convention for proposing Amendments, which, in either Case, shall be valid to all Intents and Purposes, as Part of this Constitution, when ratified by the Legislatures of three fourths of the several States, or by Conventions in three fourths thereof, as the one or the other Mode of Ratification may be proposed by the Congress; Provided that no Amendment which may be made prior to the Year One thousand eight hundred and eight shall in any Manner affect the first and fourth Clauses in the Ninth Section of the first Article; and that no State, without its Consent, shall be deprived of its equal Suffrage in the Senate.

Article. VI.

All Debts contracted and Engagements entered into, before the Adoption of this Constitution, shall be as valid against the United States under this Constitution, as under the Confederation.

This Constitution, and the Laws of the United States which shall be made in Pursuance thereof; and all Treaties made, or which shall be made, under the Authority of the United States, shall be the supreme Law of the Land; and the Judges in every State shall be bound thereby, any Thing in the Constitution or Laws of any State to the Contrary notwithstanding.

The Senators and Representatives before mentioned, and the Members of the several State Legislatures, and all executive and judicial Officers, both of the United States and of the several States, shall be bound by Oath or Affirmation, to support this Constitution; but no religious Test shall ever be required as a Qualification to any Office or public Trust under the United States.

Article. VII.

The Ratification of the Conventions of nine States, shall be sufficient for the Establishment of this Constitution between the States so ratifying the Same.

The Word, "the," being interlined between the seventh and eighth Lines of the first Page, the Word "Thirty" being partly written on an Erazure in the fifteenth Line of the first Page, The Words "is tried" being interlined between the thirty second and thirty third Lines of the first Page and the Word "the" being interlined between the forty third and forty fourth Lines of the second Page.

Attest William Jackson Secretary

done in Convention by the Unanimous Consent of the States present the Seventeenth Day of September in the Year of our Lord one thousand seven hundred and Eighty seven and of the Independance of the United States of America the Twelfth

In witness whereof We have hereunto subscribed our Names,

George Washington - President and deputy from Virginia

New Hampshire - John Langdon, Nicholas Gilman

Massachusetts - Nathaniel Gorham, Rufus King

Connecticut - William Samuel Johnson, Roger Sherman

New York - Alexander Hamilton

New Jersey - William Livingston, David Brearley, William Paterson, Jonathan Dayton

Pennsylvania - Benjamin Franklin, Thomas Mifflin, Robert Morris, George Clymer, Thomas FitzSimons, Jared Ingersoll, James Wilson, Gouvernour Morris

Delaware - George Read, Gunning Bedford Jr., John Dickinson, Richard Bassett, Jacob Broom

Maryland - James McHenry, Daniel of St Thomas Jenifer, Daniel Carroll

Virginia - John Blair, James Madison Jr.

North Carolina - William Blount, Richard Dobbs Spaight, Hugh Williamson

South Carolina - John Rutledge, Charles Cotesworth Pinckney, Charles Pinckney, Pierce Butler

Georgia - William Few, Abraham Baldwin

Attest: William Jackson, Secretary

Amendment I

Congress shall make no law respecting an establishment of religion, or prohibiting the free exercise thereof; or abridging the freedom of speech, or of the press; or the right of the people peaceably to assemble, and to petition the Government for a redress of grievances.

Amendment II

A well regulated Militia, being necessary to the security of a free State, the right of the people to keep and bear Arms, shall not be infringed.

Amendment III

No Soldier shall, in time of peace be quartered in any house, without the consent of the Owner, nor in time of war, but in a manner to be prescribed by law.

Amendment IV

The right of the people to be secure in their persons, houses, papers, and effects, against unreasonable searches and seizures, shall not be violated, and no Warrants shall issue, but upon probable cause, supported by Oath or affirmation, and particularly describing the place to be searched, and the persons or things to be seized.

Amendment V

No person shall be held to answer for a capital, or otherwise infamous crime, unless on a presentment or indictment of a Grand Jury, except in cases arising in the land or naval forces, or in the Militia, when in actual service in time of War or public danger; nor shall any person be subject for the same offence to be twice put in jeopardy of life or limb; nor shall be compelled in any criminal case to be a witness against himself, nor be deprived of life, liberty, or property, without due process of law; nor shall private property be taken for public use, without just compensation.

Amendment VI

In all criminal prosecutions, the accused shall enjoy the right to a speedy and public trial, by an impartial jury of the State and district wherein the crime shall have been committed, which district shall have been previously ascertained by law, and to be informed of the nature and cause of the accusation; to be confronted with the witnesses against him; to have compulsory process for obtaining witnesses in his favor, and to have the Assistance of Counsel for his defence.

Amendment VII

In Suits at common law, where the value in controversy shall exceed twenty dollars, the right of trial by jury shall be preserved, and no fact tried by a jury, shall be otherwise re-examined in any Court of the United States, than according to the rules of the common law.

Amendment VIII

Excessive bail shall not be required, nor excessive fines imposed, nor cruel and unusual punishments inflicted.

Amendment IX

The enumeration in the Constitution, of certain rights, shall not be construed to deny or disparage others retained by the people.

Amendment X

The powers not delegated to the United States by the Constitution, nor prohibited by it to the States, are reserved to the States respectively, or to the people.

Amendment XI

Passed by Congress March 4, 1794. Ratified February 7, 1795.

Note: Article III, section 2, of the Constitution was modified by amendment 11.

The Judicial power of the United States shall not be construed to extend to any suit in law or equity, commenced or prosecuted against one of the United States by Citizens of another State, or by Citizens or Subjects of any Foreign State.

Amendment XII

Passed by Congress December 9, 1803. Ratified June 15, 1804.

Note: A portion of Article II, section 1, of the Constitution was superseded by the 12th amendment.

The Electors shall meet in their respective states and vote by ballot for President and Vice-President, one of whom, at least, shall not be an inhabitant of the same state with themselves; they shall name in their ballots the person voted for as President, and in distinct ballots the person voted for as Vice-President, and they shall make distinct lists of all persons voted for as President, and of all persons voted for as Vice-President, and of the number of votes for each, which lists they shall sign and certify, and transmit sealed to the seat of the government of the United States, directed to the President of the Senate; — the President of the Senate shall, in the presence of the Senate and House of Representatives, open all the certificates and the votes shall then be counted; — The person having the greatest number of votes for President, shall be the President, if such number be a majority of the whole number of Electors appointed; and if no person have such majority, then from the persons having the highest numbers not exceeding three on the list of those voted for as President, the House of Representatives shall choose immediately, by ballot, the President. But in choosing the President, the votes shall be taken by states, the representation from each state having one vote; a quorum for this purpose shall consist of a member or members from two-thirds of the states, and a majority of all the states shall be necessary to a choice. [And if the House of Representatives shall not choose a President whenever the right of choice shall devolve upon them, before the fourth day of March next following, then the Vice-President shall act as President, as in case of the death or other constitutional disability of the President. —]* The person having the greatest number of votes as Vice-President, shall be the Vice-President, if such number be a majority of the whole number of Electors appointed, and if no person have a majority, then from the two highest numbers on the list, the Senate shall choose the Vice-President; a quorum for the purpose shall consist of two-thirds of the whole number of Senators, and a majority of the whole number shall be necessary to a choice. But no person constitutionally ineligible to the office of President shall be eligible to that of Vice-President of the United States.

*Superseded by section 3 of the 20th amendment.

Amendment XIII

Passed by Congress January 31, 1865. Ratified December 6, 1865.

Note: A portion of Article IV, section 2, of the Constitution was superseded by the 13th amendment.

SECTION 1.

Neither slavery nor involuntary servitude, except as a punishment for crime whereof the party shall have been duly convicted, shall exist within the United States, or any place subject to their jurisdiction.

SECTION 2.

Congress shall have power to enforce this article by appropriate legislation.

Amendment XIV

Passed by Congress June 13, 1866. Ratified July 9, 1868.

Note: Article I, section 2, of the Constitution was modified by section 2 of the 14th amendment.

SECTION 1.

All persons born or naturalized in the United States, and subject to the jurisdiction thereof, are citizens of the United States and of the State wherein they reside. No State shall make or enforce any law which shall abridge the privileges or immunities of citizens of the United States; nor shall any State deprive any person of life, liberty, or property, without due process of law; nor deny to any person within its jurisdiction the equal protection of the laws.

SECTION 2.

Representatives shall be apportioned among the several States according to their respective numbers, counting the whole number of persons in each State, excluding Indians not taxed. But when the right to vote at any election for the choice of electors for President and Vice-President of the United States, Representatives in Congress, the Executive and Judicial officers of a State, or the members of the Legislature thereof, is denied to any of the male inhabitants of such State, being twenty-one years of age,* and citizens of the United States, or in any way abridged, except for participation in rebellion, or other crime, the basis of representation therein shall be reduced in the proportion which the number of such male citizens shall bear to the whole number of male citizens twenty-one years of age in such State.

SECTION 3.

No person shall be a Senator or Representative in Congress, or elector of President and Vice-President, or hold any office, civil or military, under the United States, or under any State, who, having previously taken an oath, as a member of Congress, or as an officer of the United States, or as a member of any State legislature, or as an executive or judicial officer of any State, to support the Constitution of the United States, shall have engaged in insurrection or rebellion against the same, or given aid or comfort to the enemies thereof. But Congress may by a vote of two-thirds of each House, remove such disability.

SECTION 4.

The validity of the public debt of the United States, authorized by law, including debts incurred for payment of pensions and bounties for services in suppressing insurrection or rebellion, shall not be questioned. But neither the United States nor any State shall assume or pay any debt or obligation incurred in aid of insurrection or rebellion against the United States, or any claim for the loss or emancipation of any slave; but all such debts, obligations and claims shall be held illegal and void.

SECTION 5.

The Congress shall have the power to enforce, by appropriate legislation, the provisions of this article.

*Changed by section 1 of the 26th amendment.

Amendment XV

Passed by Congress February 26, 1869. Ratified February 3, 1870.

SECTION 1.

The right of citizens of the United States to vote shall not be denied or abridged by the United States or by any State on account of race, color, or previous condition of servitude—

SECTION 2.

The Congress shall have the power to enforce this article by appropriate legislation.

Amendment XVI

Passed by Congress July 2, 1909. Ratified February 3, 1913.

Note: Article I, section 9, of the Constitution was modified by amendment 16.

The Congress shall have power to lay and collect taxes on incomes, from whatever source derived, without apportionment among the several States, and without regard to any census or enumeration.

Amendment XVII

Passed by Congress May 13, 1912. Ratified April 8, 1913.

Note: Article I, section 3, of the Constitution was modified by the 17th amendment.

The Senate of the United States shall be composed of two Senators from each State, elected by the people thereof, for six years; and each Senator shall have one vote. The electors in each State shall have the qualifications requisite for electors of the most numerous branch of the State legislatures.

When vacancies happen in the representation of any State in the Senate, the executive authority of such State shall issue writs of election to fill such vacancies: Provided, That the legislature of any State may empower the executive thereof to make temporary appointments until the people fill the vacancies by election as the legislature may direct.

This amendment shall not be so construed as to affect the election or term of any Senator chosen before it becomes valid as part of the Constitution.

Amendment XVIII

Passed by Congress December 18, 1917. Ratified January 16, 1919. Repealed by amendment 21.

SECTION 1.

After one year from the ratification of this article the manufacture, sale, or transportation of intoxicating liquors within, the importation thereof into, or the exportation thereof from the United States and all territory subject to the jurisdiction thereof for beverage purposes is hereby prohibited.

SECTION 2.

The Congress and the several States shall have concurrent power to enforce this article by appropriate legislation.

SECTION 3.

This article shall be inoperative unless it shall have been ratified as an amendment to the Constitution by the legislatures of the several States, as provided in the Constitution, within seven years from the date of the submission hereof to the States by the Congress.

Amendment XIX

Passed by Congress June 4, 1919. Ratified August 18, 1920.

The right of citizens of the United States to vote shall not be denied or abridged by the United States or by any State on account of sex.

Congress shall have power to enforce this article by appropriate legislation.

Amendment XX

Passed by Congress March 2, 1932. Ratified January 23, 1933.

Note: Article I, section 4, of the Constitution was modified by section 2 of this amendment. In addition, a portion of the 12th amendment was superseded by section 3.

SECTION 1.

The terms of the President and the Vice President shall end at noon on the 20th day of January, and the terms of Senators and Representatives at noon on the 3d day of January, of the years in which such terms would have ended if this article had not been ratified; and the terms of their successors shall then begin.

SECTION 2.

The Congress shall assemble at least once in every year, and such meeting shall begin at noon on the 3d day of January, unless they shall by law appoint a different day.

SECTION 3.

If, at the time fixed for the beginning of the term of the President, the President elect shall have died, the Vice President elect shall become President. If a President shall not have been chosen before the time fixed for the beginning of his term, or if the President elect shall have failed to qualify, then the Vice President elect shall act as President until a President shall have qualified; and the Congress may by law provide for the case wherein neither a President elect nor a Vice President shall have qualified, declaring who shall then act as President, or the manner in which one who is to act shall be selected, and such person shall act accordingly until a President or Vice President shall have qualified.

SECTION 4.

The Congress may by law provide for the case of the death of any of the persons from whom the House of Representatives may choose a President whenever the right of choice shall have devolved upon them, and for the case of the death of any of the persons from whom the Senate may choose a Vice President whenever the right of choice shall have devolved upon them.

SECTION 5.

Sections 1 and 2 shall take effect on the 15th day of October following the ratification of this article.

SECTION 6.

This article shall be inoperative unless it shall have been ratified as an amendment to the Constitution by the legislatures of three-fourths of the several States within seven years from the date of its submission.

Amendment XXI

Passed by Congress February 20, 1933. Ratified December 5, 1933.

SECTION 1.

The eighteenth article of amendment to the Constitution of the United States is hereby repealed.

SECTION 2.

The transportation or importation into any State, Territory, or Possession of the United States for delivery or use therein of intoxicating liquors, in violation of the laws thereof, is hereby prohibited.

SECTION 3.

This article shall be inoperative unless it shall have been ratified as an amendment to the Constitution by conventions in the several States, as provided in the Constitution, within seven years from the date of the submission hereof to the States by the Congress.

Amendment XXII

Passed by Congress March 21, 1947. Ratified February 27, 1951.

SECTION 1.

No person shall be elected to the office of the President more than twice, and no person who has held the office of President, or acted as President, for more than two years of a term to which some other person was elected President shall be elected to the office of President more than once. But this Article shall not apply to any person holding the office of President when this Article was proposed by Congress, and shall not prevent any person who may be holding the office of President, or acting as President, during the term within which this Article becomes operative from holding the office of President or acting as President during the remainder of such term.

SECTION 2.

This article shall be inoperative unless it shall have been ratified as an amendment to the Constitution by the legislatures of three-fourths of the several States within seven years from the date of its submission to the States by the Congress.

Amendment XXIII

Passed by Congress June 16, 1960. Ratified March 29, 1961.

SECTION 1.

The District constituting the seat of Government of the United States shall appoint in such manner as Congress may direct:

A number of electors of President and Vice President equal to the whole number of Senators and Representatives in Congress to which the District would be entitled if it were a State, but in no event more than the least populous State; they shall be in addition to those appointed by the States, but they shall be considered, for the purposes of the election of President and Vice President, to be electors appointed by a State; and they shall meet in the District and perform such duties as provided by the twelfth article of amendment.

SECTION 2.

The Congress shall have power to enforce this article by appropriate legislation.

Amendment XXIV

Passed by Congress August 27, 1962. Ratified January 23, 1964.

SECTION 1.

The right of citizens of the United States to vote in any primary or other election for President or Vice President, for electors for President or Vice President, or for Senator or Representative in Congress, shall not be denied or abridged by the United States or any State by reason of failure to pay poll tax or other tax.

SECTION 2.

The Congress shall have power to enforce this article by appropriate legislation.

Amendment XXV

Passed by Congress July 6, 1965. Ratified February 10, 1967.

Note: Article II, section 1, of the Constitution was affected by the 25th amendment.

SECTION 1.

In case of the removal of the President from office or of his death or resignation, the Vice President shall become President.

SECTION 2.

Whenever there is a vacancy in the office of the Vice President, the President shall nominate a Vice President who shall take office upon confirmation by a majority vote of both Houses of Congress.

SECTION 3.

Whenever the President transmits to the President pro tempore of the Senate and the Speaker of the House of Representatives his written declaration that he is unable to discharge the powers and duties of his office, and until he transmits to them a written declaration to the contrary, such powers and duties shall be discharged by the Vice President as Acting President.

SECTION 4.

Whenever the Vice President and a majority of either the principal officers of the executive departments or of such other body as Congress may by law provide, transmit to the President pro tempore of the Senate and the Speaker of the House of Representatives their written declaration that the President is unable to discharge the powers and duties of his office, the Vice President shall immediately assume the powers and duties of the office as Acting President.

Thereafter, when the President transmits to the President pro tempore of the Senate and the Speaker of the House of Representatives his written declaration that no inability exists, he shall resume the powers and duties of his office unless the Vice President and a majority of either the principal officers of the executive department or of such other body as Congress may by law provide, transmit within four days to the President pro tempore of the Senate and the Speaker of the House of Representatives their written declaration that the President is unable to discharge the powers and duties of his office. Thereupon Congress shall decide the issue, assembling within forty-eight hours for that purpose if not in session. If the Congress, within twenty-one days after receipt of the latter written declaration, or, if Congress is not in session, within twenty-one days after Congress is required to assemble, determines by two-thirds vote of both Houses that the President is unable to discharge the powers and duties of his office, the Vice President shall continue to discharge the same as Acting President; otherwise, the President shall resume the powers and duties of his office.

Amendment XXVI

Passed by Congress March 23, 1971. Ratified July 1, 1971.

Note: Amendment 14, section 2, of the Constitution was modified by section 1 of the 26th amendment.

SECTION 1.

The right of citizens of the United States, who are eighteen years of age or older, to vote shall not be denied or abridged by the United States or by any State on account of age.

SECTION 2.

The Congress shall have power to enforce this article by appropriate legislation.

Amendment XXVII

Originally proposed Sept. 25, 1789. Ratified May 7, 1992.

No law, varying the compensation for the services of the Senators and Representatives, shall take effect, until an election of representatives shall have intervened.

The Articles of Confederation and Perpetual Union*

Agreed to by Congress November 15, 1777; ratified and in force, March 1, 1781.

Preamble

To all to whom these Presents shall come, we the undersigned Delegates of the States affixed to our Names send greeting.

Whereas the Delegates of the United States of America in Congress assembled did on the fifteenth day of November in the Year of our Lord One Thousand Seven Hundred and Seventy seven, and in the Second Year of the Independence of America, agree to certain articles of Confederation and perpetual Union between the States of New Hampshire, Massachusetts-bay, Rhode Island and Providence Plantations, Connecticut, New York, New Jersey, Pennsylvania, Delaware, Maryland, Virginia, North Carolina, South Carolina and Georgia, in the words following, viz:

Articles of Confederation and perpetual Union between the States of New Hampshire, Massachusetts-bay, Rhode Island and Providence Plantations, Connecticut, New York, New Jersey, Pennsylvania, Delaware, Maryland, Virginia, North Carolina, South Carolina and Georgia.

---

* *Source*: Our Documents, a joint website maintained by the National Archives and Records Administration, National History Day, and USA Freedom Corps, www.ourdocuments.gov/doc .php?flash=true&doc=3&page=transcript.

Article I.

The Stile of this Confederacy shall be "The United States of America."

Article II.

Each state retains its sovereignty, freedom, and independence, and every Power, Jurisdiction, and right, which is not by this confederation expressly delegated to the United States, in Congress assembled.

Article III.

The said States hereby severally enter into a firm league of friendship with each other, for their common defense, the security of their liberties, and their mutual and general welfare, binding themselves to assist each other, against all force offered to, or attacks made upon them, or any of them, on account of religion, sovereignty, trade, or any other pretense whatever.

Article IV.

The better to secure and perpetuate mutual friendship and intercourse among the people of the different States in this union, the free inhabitants of each of these States, paupers, vagabonds, and fugitives from justice excepted, shall be entitled to all privileges and immunities of free citizens in the several States; and the people of each State shall have free ingress and regress to and from any other State, and shall enjoy therein all the privileges of trade and commerce, subject to the same duties, impositions, and restrictions as the inhabitants thereof respectively, provided that such restrictions shall not extend so far as to prevent the removal of property imported into any State, to any other State, of which the owner is an inhabitant; provided also that no imposition, duties or restriction shall be laid by any State, on the property of the united States, or either of them.

If any person guilty of, or charged with, treason, felony, or other high misdemeanor in any State, shall flee from justice, and be found in any of the united States, he shall, upon demand of the Governor or executive power of the State from which he fled, be delivered up and removed to the State having jurisdiction of his offense.

Full faith and credit shall be given in each of these States to the records, acts, and judicial proceedings of the courts and magistrates of every other State.

Article V.

For the most convenient management of the general interests of the united States, delegates shall be annually appointed in such manner as the legislatures of each State shall direct, to meet in Congress on the first Monday in November, in every year, with a power reserved to each State to recall its delegates, or any of them, at any time within the year, and to send others in their stead for the remainder of the year.

No State shall be represented in Congress by less than two, nor more than seven members; and no person shall be capable of being a delegate for more than three years in any term of six years; nor shall any person, being a delegate, be capable of holding any office under the united States, for which he, or another for his benefit, receives any salary, fees or emolument of any kind.

Each State shall maintain its own delegates in a meeting of the States, and while they act as members of the committee of the States.

In determining questions in the united States, in Congress assembled, each State shall have one vote.

Freedom of speech and debate in Congress shall not be impeached or questioned in any court or place out of Congress, and the members of Congress shall be protected in their persons from arrests or imprisonments, during the time of their going to and from, and attendance on Congress, except for treason, felony, or breach of the peace.

Article VI.

No State, without the consent of the united States in Congress assembled, shall send any embassy to, or receive any embassy from, or enter into any conference, agreement, alliance or treaty with any King, Prince or State; nor shall any person holding any office of profit or trust under the united States, or any of them, accept any present, emolument, office or title of any kind whatever from any King, Prince or foreign State; nor shall the United States in congress assembled, or any of them, grant any title of nobility.

No two or more States shall enter into any treaty, confederation or alliance whatever between them, without the consent of the united States in congress assembled, specifying accurately the purposes for which the same is to be entered into, and how long it shall continue.

No State shall lay any imposts or duties, which may interfere with any stipulations in treaties, entered into by the united States in congress assembled, with any King, Prince or State, in pursuance of any treaties already proposed by congress, to the courts of France and Spain.

No vessel of war shall be kept up in time of peace by any State, except such number only, as shall be deemed necessary by the united States in congress assembled, for the defense of such State, or its trade; nor shall any body of forces be kept up by any State in time of peace, except such number only, as in the judgement of the united States, in congress assembled, shall be deemed requisite to garrison the forts necessary for the defense of such State; but every State shall always keep up a well-regulated and disciplined militia, sufficiently armed and accoutered, and shall provide and constantly have ready for use, in public stores, a due number of field pieces and tents, and a proper quantity of arms, ammunition and camp equipage.

No State shall engage in any war without the consent of the united States in congress assembled, unless such State be actually invaded by enemies, or shall have received certain advice of a resolution being formed by some nation of Indians to invade such State, and the danger is so imminent as not to admit of a delay till the united States in congress assembled can be consulted; nor shall any State grant commissions to any ships or vessels of war, nor letters of marque or reprisal, except it be after a declaration of war by the united States in congress assembled, and then only against the kingdom or State and the subjects thereof, against which war has been so declared, and under such regulations as shall be established by the united States in congress assembled, unless such State be infested by pirates, in which case vessels of war may be fitted out for that occasion, and kept so long as the danger shall continue, or until the united States in congress assembled shall determine otherwise.

Article VII.

When land forces are raised by any State for the common defense, all officers of or under the rank of colonel, shall be appointed by the legislature of each State respectively, by whom such forces shall be raised, or in such manner as such State shall direct, and all vacancies shall be filled up by the State which first made the appointment.

Article VIII.

All charges of war, and all other expenses that shall be incurred for the common defense or general welfare, and allowed by the united States in congress assembled, shall be defrayed out of a common treasury, which shall be supplied by the several States in proportion to the value of all land within each State, granted or surveyed for any person, as such land and the buildings and improvements thereon shall be estimated according to such mode as the united States in congress assembled, shall from time to time direct and appoint.

The taxes for paying that proportion shall be laid and levied by the authority and direction of the legislatures of the several States within the time agreed upon by the united States in congress assembled.

Article IX.

The united States in congress assembled, shall have the sole and exclusive right and power of determining on peace and war, except in the cases mentioned in the sixth article—of sending and receiving ambassadors—entering into treaties and alliances, provided that no treaty of commerce shall be made whereby the legislative power of the respective States shall be restrained from imposing such imposts and duties on foreigners, as their own people are subjected to, or from prohibiting the exportation or importation of any species of goods or commodities whatsoever—of establishing rules for deciding in all cases, what captures on land or water shall be legal, and in what manner prizes taken by land or naval forces in the service of the United States shall be divided or appropriated—of granting letters of marque and reprisal in times of peace—appointing courts for the trial of piracies and felonies committed on the high seas and establishing courts for receiving and determining finally appeals in all cases of captures, provided that no member of Congress shall be appointed a judge of any of the said courts.

The United States in Congress assembled shall also be the last resort on appeal in all disputes and differences now subsisting or that hereafter may arise between two or more States concerning boundary, jurisdiction or any other causes whatever; which authority shall always be exercised in the manner following. Whenever the legislative or executive authority or lawful agent of any State in controversy with another shall present a petition to Congress stating the matter in question and praying for a hearing, notice thereof shall be given by order of Congress to the legislative or executive authority of the other State in controversy, and a day assigned for the appearance of the parties by their lawful agents, who shall then be directed to appoint by joint consent, commissioners or judges to constitute a court for hearing and determining the matter in question: but if they cannot agree, Congress shall name three persons out of each of the United States, and from the list of such persons each party shall alternately strike out one, the petitioners beginning, until the number shall be reduced to thirteen; and from that number not less than seven, nor more than nine names as Congress shall direct, shall in the presence of Congress be drawn out by lot, and the persons whose names shall be so drawn or any five of them, shall be commissioners or judges, to hear and finally determine the controversy, so always as a major part of the judges who shall hear the cause shall agree in the determination: and if either party shall neglect to attend at the day appointed, without showing reasons, which Congress shall judge sufficient, or being present shall refuse to strike, the Congress shall proceed to nominate three persons out of each State, and the secretary of Congress shall strike in behalf of such party absent or refusing; and the judgement and sentence of the court to be appointed, in the manner before prescribed, shall be final and conclusive; and if any of the parties shall refuse to submit to the authority of such court, or to appear or defend their claim or cause, the court shall nevertheless proceed to pronounce sentence, or judgement, which shall in like manner be final and decisive, the judgement or sentence and other proceedings being in either case transmitted to Congress, and lodged among the acts of Congress for the security of the parties concerned: provided that every commissioner, before he sits in judgement, shall take an oath to be administered by one of the judges of the supreme or superior court of the State, where the cause shall be tried, 'well and truly to hear and determine the matter in question, according to the best of his judgement, without favor, affection or hope of reward': provided also, that no State shall be deprived of territory for the benefit of the United States.

All controversies concerning the private right of soil claimed under different grants of two or more States, whose jurisdictions as they may respect such lands, and the States which passed such grants are adjusted, the said grants or either of them being at the same time claimed to have originated antecedent to such settlement of jurisdiction, shall on the petition of either party to the Congress of the United States, be finally determined as near as may be in the same manner as is before prescribed for deciding disputes respecting territorial jurisdiction between different States.

The United States in Congress assembled shall also have the sole and exclusive right and power of regulating the alloy and value of coin struck by their own authority, or by that of the respective States—fixing the standards of weights and measures throughout the United States—regulating the trade and managing all affairs with the Indians, not members of any of the States, provided that the legislative right of any State within its own limits be not infringed or violated—establishing or regulating post offices from one State to another, throughout all the United States, and exacting such postage on the papers passing through the same as may be requisite to defray the expenses of the said office—appointing all officers of the land forces, in the service of the United States, excepting regimental officers—appointing all the officers of the naval forces, and commissioning all officers whatever in the service of the United States—making rules for the government and regulation of the said land and naval forces, and directing their operations.

The United States in Congress assembled shall have authority to appoint a committee, to sit in the recess of Congress, to be denominated 'A Committee of the States', and to consist of one delegate from each State; and to appoint such other committees and civil officers as may be necessary for managing the general affairs of the United States under their direction—to appoint one of their members to preside, provided that no person be allowed to serve in the office of president more than one year in any term of three years; to ascertain the necessary sums of money to be raised for the service of the United States, and to appropriate and apply the same for defraying the public expenses—to borrow money, or emit bills on the credit of the United States, transmitting every half-year to the respective States an account of the sums of money so borrowed or emitted—to build and equip a navy—to agree upon the number of land forces, and to make requisitions from each State for its quota, in proportion to the number of white inhabitants in such State; which requisition shall be binding, and thereupon the legislature of each State shall appoint the regimental officers, raise the men and cloath, arm and equip them in a solid- like manner, at the expense of the United States; and the officers and men so cloathed, armed and equipped shall march to the place appointed, and within the time agreed on by the United States in Congress assembled. But if the United States in Congress assembled shall, on consideration of circumstances judge proper that any State should not raise men, or should raise a smaller number of men than the quota thereof, such extra number shall be raised, officered, cloathed, armed and equipped in the same manner as the quota of each State, unless the legislature of such State shall judge that such extra number cannot be safely spread out in the same, in which case they shall raise, officer, cloath, arm and equip as many of such extra number as they judge can be safely spared. And the officers and men so cloathed, armed, and equipped, shall march to the place appointed, and within the time agreed on by the united States in congress assembled.

The united States in congress assembled shall never engage in a war, nor grant letters of marque or reprisal in time of peace, nor enter into any treaties or alliances, nor coin money, nor regulate the value thereof, nor ascertain the sums and expenses necessary for the defense and welfare of the United States, or any of them, nor emit bills, nor borrow money on the credit of the united States, nor appropriate money, nor agree upon the number of vessels of war, to be built or purchased, or the number of land or sea forces to be raised, nor appoint a commander in chief of the army or navy, unless nine States assent to the same: nor shall a question on any other point, except for adjourning from day to day be determined, unless by the votes of the majority of the united States in congress assembled.

The congress of the united States shall have power to adjourn to any time within the year, and to any place within the united States, so that no period of adjournment be for a longer duration than the space of six months, and shall publish the journal of their proceedings monthly, except such parts thereof relating to treaties, alliances or military operations, as in their judgement require secrecy; and the yeas and nays of the delegates of each State on any question shall be entered on the journal, when it is desired by any delegates of a State, or any of them, at his or their request shall be furnished with a transcript of the said journal, except such parts as are above excepted, to lay before the legislatures of the several States.

Article X.

The committee of the States, or any nine of them, shall be authorized to execute, in the recess of congress, such of the powers of congress as the united States in congress assembled, by the consent of the nine States, shall from time to time think expedient to vest them with; provided that no power be delegated to the said Committee, for the exercise of which, by the articles of confederation, the voice of nine States in the Congress of the United States assembled be requisite.

Article XI.

Canada acceding to this confederation, and adjoining in the measures of the united States, shall be admitted into, and entitled to all the advantages of this union; but no other colony shall be admitted into the same, unless such admission be agreed to by nine States.

Article XII.

All bills of credit emitted, monies borrowed, and debts contracted by, or under the authority of congress, before the assembling of the united States, in pursuance of the present confederation, shall be deemed and considered as a charge against the United States, for payment and satisfaction whereof the said united States, and the public faith are hereby solemnly pledged.

Article XIII.

Every State shall abide by the determination of the united States in congress assembled, on all questions which by this confederation are submitted to them. And the Articles of this confederation shall be inviolably observed by every State, and the union shall be perpetual; nor shall any alteration at any time hereafter be made in any of them; unless such alteration be agreed to in a congress of the united States, and be afterwards confirmed by the legislatures of every State.

And Whereas it hath pleased the Great Governor of the World to incline the hearts of the legislatures we respectively represent in Congress, to approve of, and to authorize us to ratify the said articles of confederation and perpetual union. Know Ye that we the undersigned delegates, by virtue of the power and authority to us given for that purpose, do by these presents, in the name and in behalf of our respective constituents, fully and entirely ratify and confirm each and every of the said articles of confederation and perpetual union, and all and singular the matters and things therein contained: And we do further solemnly plight and engage the faith of our respective constituents, that they shall abide by the determinations of the united States in congress assembled, on all questions, which by the said confederation are submitted to them. And that the articles thereof shall be inviolably observed by the States we respectively represent, and that the union shall be perpetual.

In Witness whereof we have hereunto set our hands in Congress. Done at Philadelphia in the State of Pennsylvania the ninth Day of July in the Year of our Lord one thousand seven Hundred and Seventy-eight, and in the Third Year of the independence of America.

On the part and behalf of the State of New Hampshire:

Josiah Bartlett

John Wentworth Junr. August 8th 1778

On the part and behalf of The State of Massachusetts Bay:

John Hancock

Samuel Adams

Elbridge Gerry

Francis Dana

James Lovell

Samuel Holten

On the part and behalf of the State of Rhode Island and Providence Plantations:

William Ellery

Henry Marchant

John Collins

On the part and behalf of the State of Connecticut:

Roger Sherman

Samuel Huntington

Oliver Wolcott

Titus Hosmer

Andrew Adams

On the Part and Behalf of the State of New York:

James Duane

Francis Lewis

Wm Duer

Gouv Morris

On the Part and in Behalf of the State of New Jersey, November 26, 1778.

Jno Witherspoon

Nath. Scudder

On the part and behalf of the State of Pennsylvania:

Robt Morris

Daniel Roberdeau

John Bayard Smith

William Clingan

Joseph Reed 22nd July 1778

On the part and behalf of the State of Delaware:

Tho Mckean February 12, 1779

John Dickinson May 5th 1779

Nicholas Van Dyke

On the part and behalf of the State of Maryland:

John Hanson March 1 1781

Daniel Carroll

On the Part and Behalf of the State of Virginia:

Richard Henry Lee

John Banister

Thomas Adams

Jno Harvie

Francis Lightfoot Lee

On the part and Behalf of the State of No Carolina:

John Penn July 21st 1778

Corns Harnett

Jno Williams

On the part and behalf of the State of South Carolina:

Henry Laurens

William Henry Drayton

Jno Mathews

Richd Hutson

Thos Heyward Junr

On the part and behalf of the State of Georgia:

Jno Walton 24th July 1778

Edwd Telfair

Edwd Langworthy

Notes

Introduction

1. W. Cleon Skousen, *The Making of America: The Substance and Meaning of the Constitution*, 3rd ed. (Malta, ID: National Center for Constitutional Studies, 2007), 733.

2. Think Progress, *What Happens If the Tea Party Wins*, video, September 16, 2011, www.youtube.com/watch?v=utS3LB58Z50.

3. Ibid.

4. "Justice Scalia on the Record," CBS News, February 11, 2009, www .cbsnews.com/2100-18560_162-4040290.html?tag=contentMain;contentBody.

5. *USA Today*, "Scalia on Election Ads: Turn Off the TV," January 21, 2012, www.usatoday.com/news/washington/story/2012-01-21/super-pac-scalia/52725476/1.

6. Debra Cassens Weiss, "U.S. Supreme Court: Critics 'Seem Bent on Undermining' Supreme Court, Justice Thomas Says," *American Bar Association Journal*, February 28, 2011, www.abajournal.com/news/article/critics_seem_bent_on_undermining_supreme_court_justice_thomas_says.

7. Steve Benen, "McConnell Touts BBA, Forgets the 90s," Political Animal Blog, *The Washington Monthly*, July 13, 2011, www.washingtonmonthly.com/political-animal/2011_07/mcconnell_touts_bba_forgets_th030838.php.

8. "What Happens If the Tea Party Wins? The Conservative Effort to Make Everything Unconstitutional," Center for American Progress, September 16, 2011, www.americanprogress.org/events/2011/09/constitution.html.

9. Ibid.

10. Michael Falcone, "The Note: Rick Perry on Ben Bernanke: It Would Be 'Almost Treasonous' to Print More Money between Now and the Election," ABCNews.com, August 15, 2011, https://myub.ubalt.edu/dana-na/auth/url_10/welcome.cgi.

11. Michael Barkun, *Religion and the Racist Right: The Origins of the Christian Identity Movement* (Chapel Hill: University of North Carolina Press, 1994).

12. Think Progress, *What Happens If the Tea Party Wins*.

13. PolitiFact Florida, "Allen West Says about 80 House Democrats Are Members of the Communist Party," www.politifact.com/florida/statements/2012/apr/11/allen-west/allen-west-says-about-80-house-democrats-are-membe.

14. Kevin R. C. Gutzman, *The Politically Incorrect Guide™ to the Constitution* (New York: Regnery, 2007), 127–28.

15. Eric Eckholm, "Using History to Mold Ideas on the Right," *New York Times*, May 4, 2011, www.nytimes.com/2011/05/05/us/politics/05barton.html?_r=1&ref=religionandbelief&pagewanted=print.

16. Richard A. Epstein, *How Progressives Rewrote the Constitution* (Washington, DC: Cato Institute, 2006).

17. Rick Perry, *Fed Up! Our Fight to Save America from Washington* (New York: Little, Brown, 2010), 37.

18. Andrew Napolitano, "The Rise and Fall of the Progressive Era," *Fox Business*, June 21, 2011, www.foxbusiness.com/on-air/freedom-watch/2011/06/21/rise-and-fall-progressive-era.

19. Kathleen Hall Jamieson and Joseph N. Cappella, *Echo Chamber: Rush Limbaugh and the Conservative Media Establishment* (New York: Oxford University Press, 2008).

20. Jill Lepore, *The Whites of Their Eyes: The Tea Party's Revolution and the Battle over American History* (Princeton, NJ: Princeton University Press, 2010), 16.

21. The Young Turks, "Herman Cain Fails on Constitution," May 23, 2011, www.youtube.com/watch?v=QrGyymtped8.

Chapter 1: The Right Is "Originalist"; Everyone Else Is "Idiotic"

1. "Scalia Blasts Advocates of 'Living Constitution,'" *MSNBC.com*, February 14, 2006, www.msnbc.msn.com/id/11346274/ns/us_news-life/.

2. The Federalist Society, "President George W. Bush Address 11-15-07," www.youtube.com/watch?v=6V2ij914uyc.

3. David F. Forte, "The Originalist Perspective," in *The Heritage Guide to the Constitution*, ed. Edwin Meese et al. (Washington, DC: The Heritage Foundation, 2005), 13.

4. Jaroslav Pelikan, *Interpreting the Bible and the Constitution* (New Haven, CT: Yale University Press, 2004), 100–102.

5. Leander Whitcomb Munhall, "Inspiration," in *The Fundamentals: The Famous Sourcebook of Biblical Truths*, ed. R. A. Torry et al., 2nd ed. (Grand Rapids, MI: Kregel Publications, 1990), 159, 168.

6. Dyson Hague, "The History of the Higher Criticism," in Torry et al., *Fundamentals*, 16.

7. Pauline Maier, *Ratification: The People Debate the Constitution, 1787–1788* (New York: Simon & Schuster, 2010), 83–84.

8. Anthony A. Peacock, *How to Read the Federalist Papers* (Washington, DC: The Heritage Foundation, 2010), 5.

9. Ibid., 81.

10. *Dred Scott v. Sandford*, 60 U.S. 393, 409, 15 L. Ed. 691 (1856).

11. *Brown v. Entertainment Merchants Association*, 131 S. Ct. 2729, 2752 (2011) (Thomas, J., dissenting).

12. *Citizens United v. Federal Elections Commission*, 130 S. Ct. 876, 926 (2010) (Scalia, J., concurring).

13. David Barton, *Original Intent: The Courts, the Constitution and Religion* (Aledo, TX: WallBuilders Press, 2001), 210.

14. *Rosenberger v. Rector and Visitors of the University of Virginia*, 515 U.S. 819, 856 (1995) (Thomas, J., concurring).

15. Alexander Hamilton, Federalist No. 34, in *Hamilton, Madison and Jay: The Federalist; with Letters of Brutus*, ed. Terence Ball (Cambridge: Cambridge University Press, 2003), 153.

16. William H. Rehnquist, "The Notion of a Living Constitution," *Texas Law Review* 54 (1976): 693, 694.

17. Gabriel J. Chin, "Why Senator John McCain Cannot Be President: Eleven Months and a Hundred Yards Short of Citizenship," *Michigan Law Review First Impressions* 107, no. 1 (2008).

Chapter 2: The "Purpose" of the Constitution Is to Limit Congress

1. Ron Paul, "Post-Primary New Hampshire Primary Remarks," *Project Vote Smart*, January 8, 2008, www.votesmart.org/public-statement/312787/post-primary-new-hampshire-primary-remarks.

2. Tom Coburn, "By Her Own Words, Kagan Will Violate Her Oath," *National Review Online*, July 20, 2010, www.nationalreview.com/bench-memos/231197/her-own-words-kagan-will-violate-her-oath/sen-tom-coburn.

3. Jim DeMint, "The Constitution of No," *National Review Online*, June 8, 2010, www.nationalreview.com/articles/229909/constitution-no/jim-demint.

4. Ibid.

5. U.S. Articles of Confederation, Art. VIII.

6. Alexander Hamilton, "The Defects of Our Present System," Letter to James Duane, September 3, 1780, in Alexander Hamilton, *Writings*, ed. Joanne B. Freeman (New York: The Library of America, 2001), 70–71.

7. George Washington, "Address to Congress on Resigning His Commission, December 23, 1783," in George Washington, *Writings*, ed. John Rhodehamel (New York: Library of America, 1997), 547.

8. George Washington, "Letter to Benjamin Harrison, January 18, 1784," in Washington, *Writings*, 552.

9. James Madison, "To George Washington, April 16, 1787," in James Madison, *Writings*, ed. Jack N. Rakove (New York: The Library of America, 1999), 81.

10. George Washington, "To John Jay, August 15, 1786," in Washington, *Writings*, 605.

11. John Jay to George Washington, January 7, 1787, in *The Founders' Constitution*, Vol. 1, Chap. 5, Doc. 15 (Chicago: University of Chicago Press, 1986). http://press-pubs.uchicago.edu/founders/documents/v1ch5s15.html.

12. James Madison, *Notes of Debates in the Federal Convention of 1787*, ed. Adrienne Koch (New York: W.W. Norton, 1966), 29–30.

13. Ibid., 31.

14. Ibid., 35.

15. *McCulloch v. Maryland*, 17 U.S. 316, 406 (1819).

16. Randy E. Barnett and Elizabeth Price Foley, "The Nuts and Bolts of the ObamaCare Ruling," *Wall Street Journal*, February 2, 2011, http://online.wsj.com/article/SB10001424052748703445904576117913097891574.html.

17. George Washington, "Letter to James Madison, November 5, 1786," in Washington, *Writings*, 621–22.

18. Alexander Hamilton, Federalist No. 23, in *The Federalist*, 106.

Chapter 3: Congress Has Stretched the Commerce Power Beyond Its Proper Limits

1. "Rand Paul's CPAC 2011 Speech," *The Daily Paul*, www.dailypaul.com/156704/rands-cpac-speech.

2. S.Hrg 111-1044, The Nomination of Elena Kagan to Be an Associate Justice of the Supreme Court of the United States, Hearing before the Committee on the

Judiciary, United States Senate, 111th Cong, 2d Sess., June 28–30 and July 1, 2010 (Serial No. J-111-98), 180.

3. *Alderman v. United States*, 562 U.S. 131 S. Ct. 700 (2011) (Thomas, J., dissenting from denial of cert.).

4. "Rand Paul on 'Maddow' Defends Criticism of Civil Rights Act, Says He Would Have Worked to Change Bill" (video), *Huffington Post*, May 20, 2010, www.huffingtonpost.com/2010/05/20/rand-paul-tells-maddow-th_n_582872 .html.

5. Garrett Epps, "Rand Paul's American Mistake: Taking 'New' for 'Unconstitutional,'" Atlantic.com, May 25, 2010, www.theatlantic.com/national/archive/ 2010/05/rand-pauls-american-mistake-taking-new-for-unconstitutional/57246/.

6. *United States v. Lopez*, 514 U.S. 549 (1995) (Thomas, J., concurring).

7. Jack M. Balkin, *Living Originalism* (Cambridge, MA: Harvard University Press, 2011), 379.

8. Akhil Reed Amar, *America's Constitution: A Biography* (New York: Random House, 2005), 107.

9. Kevin R. C. Gutzman, *The Politically Incorrect Guide™ to the Constitution* (New York: Regnery Publishing, 2007), 92.

10. *Gibbons v. Ogden*, 22 U. S. 1, 194 (1824).

11. *Lopez*, 514 U.S. 549 (1995).

12. *United States v. Morrison*, 529 U.S. 598 (2000).

Chapter 4: The Constitution Doesn't Separate Church and State

1. Ryan Creed, "Christine O'Donnell: I Dabbled in Witchcraft," ABC News, September 18, 2010, http://abcnews.go.com/News/christine-odonnell-dabbled -witchcraft/story?id=11671277#.Tr57yYDbjME.

2. Elizabeth Tenety, "Separation of Church and State Questioned by Christine O'Donnell," *44: Politics and Policy in Obama's Washington, Washington Post*, October 19, 2010, http://voices.washingtonpost.com/44/2010/10/separation-of -church-and-state.html.

3. Rush Limbaugh, "Media Twist O'Donnell-Coons Exchange on Church and State," *The Rush Limbaugh Show*, October 19, 2010, www.rushlimbaugh .com/daily/2010/10/19/media_twist_o_donnell_coons_exchange_on_church _and_state.

4. Peter Hamby, "Gingrich Blasts Secular 'Fanaticism' at Prayer Breakfast," *Political Ticker*, April 27, 2011, http://politicalticker.blogs.cnn.com/2011/04/27/ gingrich-blasts-secular-fanaticism-at-prayer-breakfast/.

5. Andy Birkey, "Bachmann to Raise Funds for Controversial Christian Punk Ministry," *Minnesota Independent*, September 30, 2009, http://minnesota -independent.com/45902/michele-bachmann-to-fundraise-for-controversial -ministry.

6. Thomas Jefferson to Messrs. Nehemiah Dodge and Others, a Committee of the Danbury Baptist Association, in the State of Connecticut, January 1, 1802, in Thomas Jefferson, *Writings: Autobiography, Notes on the State of Virginia, Public and Private Papers, Addresses, Letters*, ed. Merrill D. Peterson (New York: The Library of America, 1984), 510.

7. *Wallace v. Jaffree*, 472 U.S. 38, 92 (1985) (Rehnquist, J., dissenting).

8. Roger Williams, "Mr. Cottons Letter Lately Printed, Examined and Answered" (London, 1644), in *The Complete Writings of Roger Williams*, ed. Reuben Aldridge Guild (New York: Russell & Russell, 1963), 1:108.

9. Sydney Ahlstrom, *A Religious History of the American People* (New Haven, CT: Yale University Press, 1974), 167.

10. Ibid., 168.

11. Barton, *Orginal Intent*, 13.

12. Eric Eckholm, "Using History to Mold Ideas on the Right," *New York Times*, May 4, 2011.

13. WallBuilders, "Overview," www.wallbuilders.com/abtoverview.asp.

14. Barton, *Original Intent*, 308.

15. David Barton, *Separation of Church and State: What the Founders Meant* (Aledo, TX: WallBuilders Press, 2007), 6.

16. "A Century of Lawmaking for a New Nation: U.S. Congressional Documents and Debates, 1774–1875," http://memory.loc.gov/cgi-bin/query/ r?ammem/hlaw:@field(DOCID+@lit(hj0011)).

17. Neil H. Cogan, ed., *The Complete Bill of Rights: The Drafts, Debates, Sources, & Origins* (New York: Oxford University Press, 1997), 1–11 ("Drafts in Congress"), 53–63 ("Discussion of Drafts and Proposals: The First Congress").

18. James Madison, "Speech Proposing Constitutional Amendments," in *Writings*, ed. Jack N. Rakove (New York: Library of America, 1999), 443.

19. *The Jefferson Bible, Smithsonian Edition: The Life and Morals of Jesus of Nazareth* (Washington, DC: Smithsonian Books, 2011), back matter.

20. Letter to Dr. Benjamin Waterhouse, June 26, 1822, in *Jefferson*, 1459.

21. John Adams to Thomas Jefferson, Boston, 25 June 1813, in *The Adams-Jefferson Letters Vol. 2*, ed. Lester J. Cappon (Chapel Hill: University of North Carolina Press, 1959), 334.

22. "Treaty of Peace and Friendship, signed at Tripoli November 4, 1796 . . . and at Algiers January 3, 1797."

23. James Madison, "Memorial and Remonstrance Against Religious Assessments (1785)," in Madison, *Writings*, 31.

24. Barton, *Original Intent*, 45.

25. Ibid., 39.

26. "Affirmation," *Oxford English Dictionary*, 2nd ed. (Oxford: Oxford University Press, 1989; online version December 2011), www.oed.com/view/Entry/3423.

27. Barton, *Original Intent*, 26–27.

28. Ibid., 24.

29. Gen. 27:38.

30. *McCreary Co. v ACLU*, 545 U.S. 844, 882 (2005) (O'Connor, J., concurring).

Chapter 5: Equality and Self-Government Are "Wholly Foreign to the First Amendment"

1. *Arizona Free Enterprise Club's Freedom Club PAC v. Bennett*, 131 S. Ct. 2806 (2011).

2. Transcript of Oral Argument at 48, *Arizona Free Enterprise*, 131 S. Ct. 2806 (2011) (No. 10-238), March 28, 2011.

3. Transcript of Oral Argument at 36, *Sackett v. Environmental Protection Agency*, 566 US 132 S. Ct. 1367 (2012) (No. 10-1062), January 9, 2012.

4. *Citizens United v. Federal Election Commission*, 130 S. Ct. 876 (2010).

5. *Citizens United*, 130 S. Ct., 910.

6. *United States v. Danielczyk*, 791 F.Supp.2d 513, 518 (E.D. Va. 2001).

7. Mitch McConnell, "'Completely Wrong' on *Citizens United*," *Mitch McConnell Republican Leader, U.S. Senator for Kentucky*, January 28, 2010, http://mcconnell.senate.gov/public/index.cfm?p=PressReleases&ContentRecord_id=78607ccf-6e92-4cfb-830a-9b25d89f4632&ContentType_id=c19bc7a5-2bb9-4a73-b2ab-3c1b5191a72b&Group_id=0fd6ddca-6a05-4b26-8710-a0b7b59a8f1f.

8. Conference Blog, "Pence Praises Supreme Court Decision in *Citizens United* Case," *GOP.gov* (blog), January 21, 2010, www.gop.gov/blog/10/01/21/pence-praises-supreme-court-decision.

9. David D. Kirkpatrick, "Courts Roll Back Limits on Election Spending," *New York Times*, January 8, 2010, www.nytimes.com/2010/01/09/us/politics/09donate.html.

10. "Bringing the Courts Back Under the Constitution," NEWT 2012 Position Paper, 27, www.newt.org/sites/newt.org/files/Courts.pdf.

11. *Citizens United*, 130 S. Ct. 979 (Stevens, J., dissenting).

12. Remarks by the President in the State of the Union Address, January 27, 2010, www.whitehouse.gov/the-press-office/remarks-president-state-union-address.

13. Jeffrey D. Clements, *Corporations Are Not People: Why They Have More Rights Than You Do and What You Can Do About It* (San Francisco: Berrett-Koehler Publishers, 2012).

14. *First National Bank of Boston v. Bellotti*, 435 U.S. 765, 827 (1977) (Rehnquist, J., dissenting).

15. "Colbert Super PAC—John Paul Stevens: Retired Supreme Court Justice John Paul Stevens Expounds on His Dissenting Opinion in *Bush v. Gore* and *Citizens United*," *The Colbert Report*, January 19, 2012, www.colbertnation.com/the-colbert-report-videos/406409/january-19-2012/colbert-super-pac---john-paul-stevens.

16. *FCC v. AT&T, Inc.*, 131 S.Ct. 1177, 1185 (2011).

17. *Buckley v. Valeo*, 424 U.S. 1, 47 (1976).

18. *Federal Election Commission v. Wisconsin Right to Life, Inc.*, 551 U.S. 449, 474, 2669 (2007).

19. *Morse v. Frederick*, 551 U.S. 393, 402 (2007).

20. *Garcetti v. Ceballos*, 547 U.S. 410, 421 (2006).

21. *Lorillard Tobacco Co. v. Reilly*, 533 U.S. 525 (2001).

22. William Goldman, *The Princess Bride*, http://princessbride.8m.com/script.htm.

23. *Western Tradition Partnership v. Attorney General* (No. DA 11-0081), Slip. Op. at 13, 2011 MT 328 (Montana Supreme Court, December 20, 2011).

24. Ibid. at 11.

25. United States Supreme Court, "Order in Pending Case 11A762, *American Tradition Partnership, Inc. v. Bullock*" (February 17, 2012), www.supremecourt.gov/orders/courtorders/021712zr1.pdf.

26. Kent Greenfield, "How to Make *Citizens United* Worse," *Washington Post*, January 19, 2012.

27. *Citizens United*, 130 S. Ct. 876, 911 (2010).

Chapter 6: The Second Amendment Allows Citizens to Threaten Government

1. "Ron Paul: 'Civil Disobedience and the 2nd Amendment,'" YouTube.com (September 3, 2008), www.youtube.com/watch?v=7O7sE1f8NA8&NR=1.

2. David Kopel, "Trust the People: The Case against Gun Control," Cato Institute Policy Analysis No. 109 (1988), 25, quoted in Joshua Horwitz and Casey Anderson, *Guns, Democracy, and the Insurrectionist Idea* (Ann Arbor: University of Michigan Press, 2009), 14.

3. Andrew Belonsky, "Rand Paul, Tea Party Shoulder Blame for Head Stomp Attack," *Death and Taxes*, October 26, 2010, www.deathandtaxesmag.com/ 33792/rand-paul-tea-party-shoulder-blame-for-head-stomp-attack/.

4. Sam Stein, "Sharron Angle Floated '2nd Amendment Remedies' as 'Cure' for 'The Harry Reid Problems,'" *Huffington Post*, June 16, 2010, www .huffingtonpost.com/2010/06/16/sharron-angle-floated-2nd_n_614003.html.

5. *District of Columbia v. Heller*, 554 U.S. 570 (2008).

6. *McDonald v. City of Chicago*, 130 S.Ct. 3020 (2010).

7. J. Harvie Wilkinson III, "Of Guns, Abortions, and the Unraveling Rule of Law," *Virginia Law Review* 95, no. 253 (2009).

8. Gun Owners of America, "U.S. Senate Confirms Anti-gun Radical to the Supreme Court," August 5, 2010, http://gunowners.org/a080510.htm.

9. Virginia Attorney General, Opinion No. 11-043, Richmond, VA, April 8, 2011, www.oag.state.va.us/Opinions%20and%20Legal%20Resources/OPINIONS/ 2011opns/11-043%20cole.pdf.

10. Adam Winkler, *Gunfight: The Battle over the Right to Bear Arms in America* (New York: W. W. Norton, 2011), 83.

11. See, for example, Kentucky Coalition to Carry Concealed, "The Obvious Intent of the Second Amendment to the Constitution of the United States of America," www.kc3.com/editorial/quotes.htm; Kevin Price, "Bill of Rights Were [*sic*] Designed to Protect the People, Not the Government," *Renew America*, January 22, 2011, www.renewamerica.com/columns/price/110122; Austin Raynor, "Gun Rights as a Defense against Tyranny," *The Libertarian Solution*, November 30, 2009, www.libertariansolution.com/liberty-library/025/gun-rights-as-a-defense -against-tyranny; Davis Patterson, "UN Counts on Peaceful Submission," Letters to the Editor, *News of Cumberland County* [N.J.], February 21, 2012, www.nj.com/ cumberland/voices/index.ssf/2012/02/un_counts_on_peaceful_submissi.html.

12. Monticello Foundation, "Spurious Quotations, 'When governments fear the people, there is liberty. . . .' (Quotation)," www.monticello.org/site/jefferson/ when-governments-fear-people-there-libertyquotation#_note-2.

13. "Barnhill-Tichenor Debate on Socialism," *Rip-Saw Library No. 101* (1914), 34 (http://debs.indstate.edu/b262b3_1914.pdf).

14. Garrett Epps, "Constitutional Myth #6: The Second Amendment Allows Citizens to Threaten Government," Atlantic.com, June 20, 2011, www.theatlantic .com/national/archive/2011/06/constitutional-myth-6-the-second-amendment -allows-citizens-to-threaten-government/241298/.

15. Winkler, *Gunfight*, 114.

16. Madison, *Notes of Debates*, 241.

17. George Washington, "Sixth Annual Message to Congress," November 19, 1794, in Washington, *Writings*, 891.

18. Akhil Reed Amar, *The Bill of Rights: Creation and Reconstruction* (New Haven, CT: Yale University Press), 258.

19. KMBC, "Gun Target Stickers Found at Mo. Senate Offices," January 24, 2012, www.kmbc.com/news/30290617/detail.html#ixzz1m6lX1Nz0.

20. Brian McNeil, "Severed Gas Line Found at Home of Perriello Brother," *Daily Progress*, March 24, 2010, www2.dailyprogress.com/news/cdp-news-local/2010/mar/24/damage_at_home_of_perriello_brother_under_investig-ar-75186.

21. Anita Kumar, "Richmond Police Investigate Shot Fired at Cantor's Office," *Washington Post*, March 25, 2010, http://voices.washingtonpost.com/virginiapolitics/2010/03/richmond_pd_investigating_cant.html.

Chapter 7: The Tenth Amendment Protects "States' Rights" and "State Sovereignty"

1. James C. McKinley Jr., "Texas Governor's Secession Talk Stirs Furor," *New York Times*, April 18, 2009.

2. "Concurrent Resolution," H.C.R. No. 50, www.capitol.state.tx.us/tlodocs/81R/billtext/html/HC00050I.htm.

3. Tenth Amendment Center, "10th Amendment Resolutions," http://tenthamendmentcenter.com/nullification/10th-amendment-resolutions.

4. Ian Millhiser, "Rally 'Round the True Constitution," *American Prospect*, August 25, 2009, http://prospect.org/article/rally-round-true-constitution-0.

5. Jim DeMint, "The Constitution of No," *National Review Online*, June 8, 2010, www.nationalreview.com/articles/229909/constitution-no/jim-demint.

6. Perry, *Fed Up!*, 187–88.

7. Republican Party Iowa and *Des Moines Register*, "Mitt Romney at Iowa State Fair," *C-SPAN Video Library*, August 11, 2011, www.c-spanvideo.org/program/300933-2.

8. Michael Maharrey, "Grand Mythmaking: Debunking Garrett Epps," Tenth Amendment Center, July 15, 2011, http://tenthamendmentcenter.com/2011/07/15/grand-mythmaking-debunking-garrett-epps.

9. Leonard W. Levy, *Origins of the Bill of Rights* (New Haven, CT: Yale University Press, 1999), 23.

10. Neil H. Cogan, ed., *The Complete Bill of Rights* (New York: Oxford University Press, 1997), 683.

11. *McCulloch v. Maryland*, 17 U.S. 316, 406-07 (1819).

12. Thomas Jefferson, "Draft of the Kentucky Resolution," in Jefferson, *Writings*, 453.

13. Gordon S. Wood, *Empire of Liberty: A History of the Early Republic, 1789–1815* (Oxford: Oxford University Press, 2009), 269.

14. Ibid.

15. James Madison, "Virginia Resolutions against the Alien and Sedition Acts, December 21, 1798," in Madison, *Writings*, 591.

16. Daniel Walker Howe, *What Hath God Wrought? The Transformation of America, 1815–1848* (New York: Oxford University Press, 2007), 404.

17. James Madison, Letter to Nicholas P. Trist, December 23, 1832, in Madison, *Writings*, 862.

18. Howe, *What Hath God Wrought?*, 405–6.

19. James J. Kilpatrick, *The Sovereign States: Notes of a Citizen of Virginia* (New York: Regnery, 1957), x.

20. Ian Millhiser, "Sen. Mike Lee Calls Child Labor Laws Unconstitutional," *Think Progress*, January 14, 2011, http://thinkprogress.org/politics/2011/01/14/139049/lee-child-labor/.

21. "An Act to prevent interstate commerce in the products of child labor, and for other purposes," 64 Cong. Ch. 432, 39 Stat. 675 (September 1, 1916).

22. *United States v. Darby*, 312 U.S. 100 (1941).

23. Fair Labor Standards Act of 1938, 29 U.S.C.A. § 213(a)(6).

24. Human Rights Watch, "World Report 2010, United States," January 2010, www.hrw.org/en/node/87447.

Chapter 8: The Fourteenth Amendment Is Obsolete and Irrelevant

1. "Russell Pearce on Why the 14th Amendment Bars 'Anchor Babies,'" www.youtube.com/watch?v=cP5V84RJ5JE.

2. Theda Skocpol and Vanessa Williamson, *The Tea Party and the Remaking of Republican Conservatism* (New York: Oxford University Press, 2011), 50.

3. Skousen, *The Making of America*, 721.

4. Memorial to Congress—Fourteenth and Fifteenth Amendments to U.S. Constitution Be Declared Void (sic), Joint Resolution of the Georgia General Assembly No. 45 (Senate Resolution No. 39), March 8, 1957, http://georgiainfo.galileo.usg.edu/1957resn-7.htm.

5. "Glenn Beck, on Anchor Babies, Claims U.S. Is Only Country with Automatic Citizenship upon Birth," *Tampa Bay Times PolitiFact*, www.politifact.com/truth-o-meter/statements/2009/jun/19/glenn-beck/glenn-beck-claims-us-only-country-automatic-citize/.

6. Barton, *Original Intent*, 204.

7. Ibid.

8. Adam Cohen, "Case Study: Justice Scalia Mouths Off on Sex Discrimination," *Time*, September 22, 2010, www.time.com/time/nation/article/0,8599,2020667,00.html.

9. See Garrett Epps, *Democracy Reborn: The Fourteenth Amendment and the Fight for Equal Rights in Post–Civil War America* (New York: Henry Holt, 2006), 205–21.

10. Perry, *Fed Up!*, 96.

11. Ibid., 101.

12. Congressional Globe, 39th Congress, 1st sess., 2765.

13. Perry, *Fed Up!*, 13.

Chapter 9: Election of Senators Destroys "States' Rights"

1. Ian Millhiser, "Scalia Jumps on the Anti–Seventeenth Amendment Bandwagon," *Think Progress*, November 15, 2010, http://thinkprogress.org/politics/2010/11/15/130083/scalia-seventeenth/?mobile=nc.

2. Perry, *Fed Up!*, 38.

3. Ibid., 42.

4. Glenn Beck, *Arguing with Idiots: How to Stop Small Minds and Big Government* (New York: Threshold Editions, 2009), 215.

5. Chelsea Rudman, "Fox's Napolitano Celebrates Election Day by Promoting Taking Power from the People and Giving it to Government," *Media Matters for America*, November 2, 2010, http://mediamatters.org/blog/201011020011.

6. U.S. Senator Zell Miller: Floor Statement on Repealing the Seventeenth Amendment, April 24, 2004, www.freerepublic.com/focus/f-news/1134065/posts.

7. George F. Will, "Sen. Feingold's Constitution," *Washington Post*, February 22, 2009, www.washingtonpost.com/wp-dyn/content/article/2009/02/20/AR2009022003034.html?nav=rss_opinion/columns.

8. David Graham Phillips, *The Treason of the Senate* (1896; reprinted Chicago: Quandrangle Books, 1964), 59.

9. George Henry Haynes, *The Election of Senators* (New York: Henry Holt, 1912), 49.

10. Thomas Woods, *Nullification: How to Resist Federal Tyranny in the 21st Century* (New York: Regnery, 2010), 127.

11. James Madison, Federalist No. 10, *The Federalist*, 44.

12. Glenn Beck, "James Madison and the Seventeenth Amendment," June 12, 2010, www.glennbeck.com/content/articles/article/198/41793/.

Chapter 10: International Law Is a Threat to the Constitution

1. Sandy Adams, "Adams: Ban Foreign Law from Courts," *Washington Times*, March 9, 2011, www.washingtontimes.com/news/2011/mar/9/in-recent-years -supreme-court-justices-have-interj.

2. *Atkins v. Virginia*, 536 U.S. 304 (2002).

3. *Roper v. Simmons*, 543 U.S. 551 (2005).

4. *Lawrence v. Texas*, 539 U.S. 558 (2003).

5. Ballotpedia, "Oklahoma International Law Amendment (2010), Constitutional changes," http://ballotpedia.us/wiki/index.php/Oklahoma_International_ Law_Amendment_(2010),_Constitutional_changes.

6. Confirmation Hearing on the Nomination of the Hon. Sonia Sotomayor, Hearing before the Committee on the Judiciary, United States Senate, 111th Cong., 1st Sess., July 13–16, 2009, 132.

7. *Hamdi v. Rumsfeld*, 542 U.S. 507 (2004).

8. S. Hrg 111-1044, The Nomination of Elena Kagan to Be an Associate Justice of the Supreme Court of the United States, Hearing before the Committee on the Judiciary, United States Senate, 111th Cong, 2nd Sess. (2010), 127.

9. Transcript of Discussion between U.S. Supreme Court Justices Antonin Scalia and Stephen Breyer, American University Washington College of Law, http://domino.american.edu/AU/media/mediarel.nsf/1D265343BDC21897852 56B810071F238/1F2F7DC4757FD01E85256F890068E6E0?OpenDocument (January 13, 2005).

10. Madison, *Notes of Debates*, 337.

11. Ibid., 637.

12. John Jay, Federalist No. 3, *The Federalist*, 10.

13. George Washington, "Proclamation of Neutrality, April 22, 1793," in Washington, *Writings*, 840.

14. *Atkins*, 536 U.S. 304, 316, n.21 (2002).

15. *Roper*, 543 U.S. 551, 577 (2005).

16. Ibid.

17. Ibid., 624 (Scalia, J., dissenting).

18. "Unusual," *Oxford English Dictionary*, 2nd ed. (Oxford: Oxford University Press, 1989; online version September 2011), www.oed.com/view/Entry/219255 (accessed December 5, 2011).

19. *Bowers v. Hardwick*, 478 U.S. 186, 196 (1986) (Burger, C. J., concurring).

20. *Thompson v. Oklahoma*, 487 U.S. 815, 868 n. 4 (Scalia, J., dissenting).

21. Gordon Wood, "Introduction," in *The Idea of America: Reflections on the Birth of the United States* (New York: Penguin, 2011), 2–3.

22. Ibid., 279.

23. Charles M. Blow, "Santorum's Gospel of Inequality," *New York Times*, February 17, 2012.

24. *Awad v. Ziriax*, No. 10-6273, 670 F.3d 111 (10th Cir. 2012).

25. Robert Bolt, *A Man for All Seasons: A Play of Thomas More* (Portsmouth, NH: Heinemann, 1996), 39.

Afterword: The Battle Ahead

1. Thomas Jefferson, "Patience and the Reign of Witches," Thomas Jefferson to John Taylor, June 4, 1798, in Jefferson, *Writings*, 1048.

2. Thomas Paine, "The American Crisis, Number 1," in *Collected Writings*, ed. Eric Foner (New York: The Library of America, 1995), 91.

3. Sinclair Lewis, *It Can't Happen Here* (1935, reprinted New York: New American Library, 2005), 357.

4. Samuel Johnson, "The Rambler No. 8 (Saturday, 14 April 1750)," in Samuel Johnson, *Selected Poetry and Prose*, ed. Frank Brady and W. K. Wimsatt (Berkeley: University of California Press, 1977), 161.

Suggestions for Further Reading

The Text

The Constitution of the United States of America, Analysis and Interpretation: Analysis of Cases Decided by the Supreme Court of the United States, http://www .gpoaccess.gov/constitution/browse2002.html#2002.

Philip Kurland and Ralph Lerner, *The Founders' Constitution* (Chicago: University of Chicago Press), http://press-pubs.uchicago.edu/founders/.

The Founders in Their Own Words

John Adams, *Revolutionary Writings, 1755–1775* and *Revolutionary Writings, 1775–1783,* ed. Gordon Wood (New York: Library of America, 2011).

John Adams and Thomas Jefferson, *The Adams-Jefferson Letters: The Complete Correspondence between Thomas Jefferson and Abigail and John Adams,* ed. Lester J. Cappon (Chapel Hill: University of North Carolina Press, 1988).

Alexander Hamilton, *Writings,* ed. Joanne B. Freeman (New York: Library of America, 2001).

Alexander Hamilton, John Jay, and James Madison, *The Federalist with Letters of Brutus,* ed. Terence Ball (New York: Cambridge University Press, 2003).

Thomas Jefferson, *Writings,* ed. Merrill D. Peterson (New York: Library of America, 1984).

James Madison, *Notes of Debates in the Federal Convention of 1787,* ed. Adrienne Koch (Columbus: Ohio University Press, 1985).

James Madison, *Writings,* ed. Jack N. Rakove (New York: Library of America, 1999).

George Washington, *Writings*, ed. John H. Rhodehamel (New York: Library of
America, 1997).

The Founding

Bernard Bailyn, ed., *The Debate on the Constitution*, 2 vols. (New York: Library
of America, 1993).
Richard Beeman, *Plain, Honest Men: The Making of the American Constitution*
(New York: Random House, 2010).
Pauline Maier, *American Scripture: Making the Declaration of Independence* (New
York: Vintage, 1998).
Pauline Maier, *Ratification: The People Debate the Constitution, 1787–1788* (New
York: Simon & Schuster, 2010).
Jack N. Rakove, *Original Meanings: Politics and Ideas in the Making of the Constitu-
tion* (New York: Vintage, 1997).

The Constitution Generally

Akhil Reed Amar, *America's Constitution: A Biography* (New York: Random
House, 2005).
Richard Beeman, *The Penguin Guide to the United States Constitution: A Fully
Annotated Declaration of Independence, U.S. Constitution and Amendments, and
Selections from The Federalist Papers* (New York: Penguin, 2010).

The Bill of Rights

Akhil Reed Amar, *The Bill of Rights: Creation and Reconstruction* (New Haven,
CT: Yale University Press, 2000).
Neil H. Cogan, *The Complete Bill of Rights: The Drafts, Debates, Sources and Ori-
gins* (New York: Oxford University Press, 1997).
Leonard W. Levy, *Origins of the Bill of Rights* (New Haven, CT: Yale University
Press, 1999).

Amendments

Garrett Epps, *Democracy Reborn: The Fourteenth Amendment and the Fight for Equal
Rights in Post–Civil War America* (New York: Henry Holt & Co., 2006).

Donald E. Kyvig, *Explicit and Authentic Acts: Amending the U.S. Constitution, 1776–1995* (Lawrence: University of Kansas Press, 1998).

The Supreme Court

Peter Irons, *A People's History of the Supreme Court* (New York: Viking, 1999).

Robert G. McCloskey and Sanford V. Levinson, *The American Supreme Court*, 5th ed. (Chicago: University of Chicago Press, 2010).

Jeff Sheshol, *Supreme Power: Franklin Roosevelt vs. the Supreme Court* (New York: W.W. Norton, 2010).

Jeffrey Toobin, *The Nine: Inside the Secret World of the Supreme Court* (New York: Anchor, 2008).

Constitutional Interpretation

Jack Balkin, *Living Originalism* (Cambridge, MA: Harvard University Press, 2011).

Erwin Chemerinsky, *The Conservative Assault on the Constitution* (New York: Simon & Schuster, 2010).

Leonard W. Levy, *Original Intent and the Framers' Constitution* (Lanham, MD: Ivan R. Dee, 2000).

Jack N. Rakove, ed., *Interpreting the Constitution: The Debate over Original Intent* (Evanston, IL: Northwestern University Press, 1990).

David A. Strauss, *The Living Constitution* (New York: Oxford University Press, 2010).

Index

About the Author

Garrett Epps is a journalist, novelist, and legal scholar. A former reporter for the *Washington Post*, he has written features or commentary for the *New York Times Magazine*, the *New York Times Book Review*, the *New York Review of Books*, the *Nation*, the *New Republic*, *Salon*, and *Slate*. He is the author of two critically acclaimed novels and of two works of general nonfiction about the law: *To an Unknown God: Religious Freedom on Trial* and *Democracy Reborn: The Fourteenth Amendment and the Fight for Equal Rights in Post–Civil War America*. Both were finalists for the American Bar Association's Silver Gavel Book Award for best work of legal nonfiction. *Democracy Reborn* also won the 2007 Oregon Book Award for General Nonfiction. He has taught constitutional law at American University, Boston College Law School, Duke University, and the University of Oregon. He is currently professor of law at the University of Baltimore. He lives in Washington, D.C., and has covered the Supreme Court and the Constitution as legal affairs editor for both the *Atlantic* (online) and the *American Prospect*.